Sally Morgan was born in Perth, Western Australia, in 1951. She completed a Bachelor of Arts degree at The University of Western Australia in 1974. She also has post-graduate diplomas from The Western Australian Institute of Technology (now Curtin University of Technology) in Counselling Psychology and Computing and Library Studies. She is married with three children.

As well as writing, Sally Morgan has also established a national reputation as an artist. She has works in numerous private and public collections both in Australia and North America. Her first book, *My Place*, became and instant national best-seller, and has been published to considerable acclaim in Britain and North America. *Wanamurraganya: The Story of Jack McPhee* is her second book.

Mother and Daughter

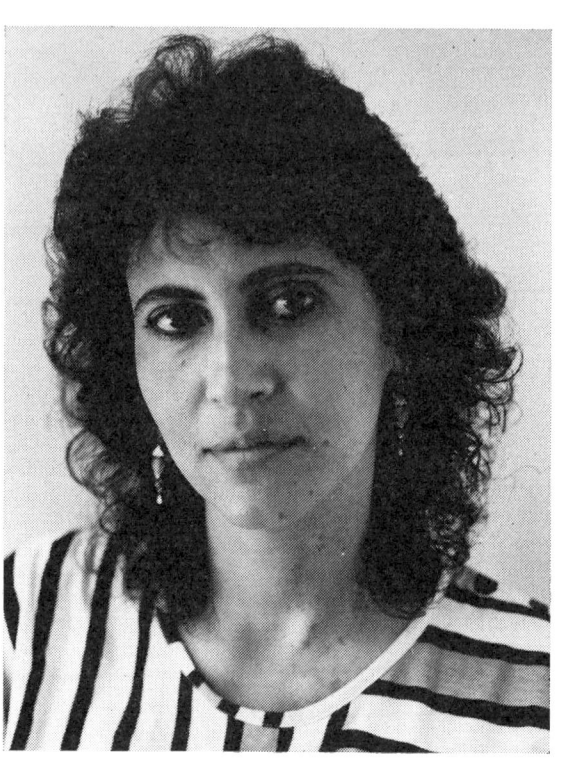

Mother and Daughter

THE STORY OF DAISY
AND GLADYS CORUNNA

SALLY MORGAN

edited by Barbara Ker Wilson

FREMANTLE ARTS CENTRE PRESS

First published 1990 by
FREMANTLE ARTS CENTRE PRESS
193 South Terrace (PO Box 320), South Fremantle
Western Australia, 6162.

Reprinted 1990, 1991, 1992, 1995.

Original unabridged edition of *My Place* published 1987.

Copyright © Sally Morgan, 1987, 1990.

This book is copyright. Apart from any fair dealing for the purpose of private study, research, criticism or review, as permitted under the Copyright Act, no part may be reproduced by any process without written permission. Enquiries should be made to the publisher.

Editor Barbara Ker Wilson.
Designed by John Douglass.
Production Manager Helen Idle.

Typeset in 11/12pt Clearface by Typestyle, Perth, Western Australia and printed on 90gsm Master Offset by Lamb Printers, Perth.

National Library of Australia
Cataloguing-in-publication data

Morgan, Sally, 1951-
  Mother and daughter: the story of Daisy and Gladys Corunna.

  ISBN 0 949206 79 2.

  1. Morgan, Sally, 1951- -Family. [2]. Aborigines,
  Australian - Biography - Juvenile Literature. [3].
  Aborigines, Australian - Women - Biography - Juvenile
  literature. [4]. Aborigines, Australian - Social life
  and customs - Juvenile literature. I. Wilson, Barbara Ker,
  1929- II. Morgan, Sally, 1951- . My Place. III
  Title. IV. Title: My Place.

994.00499 15

To My Family

How deprived we would have been
if we had been willing
to let things stay as they were.
We would have survived,
but not as a whole people.
We would never have known
our place.

ACKNOWLEDGEMENTS

Fremantle Arts Centre Press receives financial assistance from the Western Australian Department for the Arts.

Some of the personal names included in this book have been changed, or only first names included, to protect the privacy of those concerned.

CONTENTS

1	SOMEONE LIKE ME	11
2	GLADYS CORUNNA'S STORY	19
	Parkerville	19
	A Crying Tree	24
	Treats And Punishments	32
	Holidays	40
	School	43
	Change Of Scene	46
	Claremont	51
	'I'm Aboriginal'	56
	Bill's War	60
	A Road Like Mine	68
3	SOMETHING SERIOUS	78
4	GOOD NEWS	84
5	DAISY CORUNNA'S STORY	90
	Talahue	90
	Ivanhoe	100
	Arthur	103
	Gladdie	107
	'By Gee, It'd Be Good'	113
6	THE BIRD CALL	118

1

SOMEONE LIKE ME

I was fifteen when I first realised that my family was Aboriginal. Until then, I had believed I was Indian, for that was what my mother and Nan, my grandmother, had always said. I was the eldest of five children. My father died when I was nine years old, and my mother was left to bring us up. Nan, my grandmother, lived with us as well. Helen, my youngest sister, was only eighteen months when my father died. My other sister was Jill, and I had two brothers, David and Billy.

Our home was a rented house in a working-class suburb of Perth. We had a warm, loving family, all very close to one another.

I shall never forget the day I came home from school to find Nan sitting at the kitchen table, crying. I froze in the doorway. I'd never seen her cry before.

'Nan...what's wrong?' I asked.

She lifted up one arm and thumped her clenched fist hard on the table. 'You kids don't want me, you want a white grandmother. I'm black! Do you hear, black, black, black!' With that, she pushed back her chair and hurried to her room. I never did find out what had upset her so. I think it was all to do with us growing up and not being little kids any longer.

I remember how I continued to stand in the doorway. I could feel the strap of my heavy school-bag cutting into my shoulder, but I was too stunned to remove it.

For the first time in my fifteen years, I was conscious of Nan's colouring. She was right, she wasn't white. Well, I thought logically, if she wasn't white, then neither were we. What did that make us, what did that make me? I had never thought of myself as being black before.

I was very excited by my new heritage, and ever since that day I had been trying to find out more about our family. My mother wouldn't openly admit the fact that we were part-Aboriginal until I was at University — and then the truth slipped out by accident in the middle of a conversation one day. Since then, she'd become as eager as I was to find out about our people.

After I married, I still saw my family nearly every day. There were such strong bonds between us it was impossible for me not to want to see them. Just as well Paul, my husband, was the uncomplaining sort! Though in fact he fitted into our family very well. I had married Paul Morgan in 1971, while I was at University. Paul was a teacher. He had spent his childhood in the north-west of Western Australia — his parents were missionaries. When he was thirteen, they had moved to Perth to start a hostel for mission children who came to the city to attend high school. At that time, Paul spoke only pidgin English; he'd had a hard time adjusting to his new life at first. We now had three children. Our daughter, Ambelin, was born in 1975 and we had two sons — Blaze, born in 1977, and Zeke, born five years later.

In 1979 I had decided to write a book about our family history. My mother was very willing to help me, but my grandmother had always been very secretive about her past. She absolutely refused to talk about it. I knew I couldn't expect any help from her. I had already recorded the reminiscences of Nan's brother, my Great-uncle Arthur Corunna. He completed his story just before he died. I knew that he had a premonition he was about to go. He said at the end of his story: 'To live to ninety, that's an achievement...Now my life is nearly over, I'm lookin' forward to heaven... I look back on my life and think how lucky I am...I got Daisy's granddaughter [Daisy was my grandmother's name] writing my story. It should be someone in the family. It's fittin'. I want everyone to read it. Arthur Corunna's story! You see, it's important because then maybe they'll understand how hard it's been for the blackfella to live the way he wants. I'm part of history, that's how I look on it...'

It was a wonderful story, and it made Mum and me determined to continue to find out as much as we could about the family.

In 1982, when Zeke was only six weeks old, Mum, Paul and I and our children set off to visit Corunna Downs, Nan and Arthur's birthplace. They had both been taken away from their people when they were children and placed in a mission. Back in the early years of this century, that was what happened to hundreds of half-caste children. Neither Arthur nor, it seems, Daisy ever saw their Aboriginal mother, Annie Padewani, again. Nan was not really sure who her white father was, though Arthur was positive she was his full sister, and that they both had the same father, Howden Drake-Brockman, the owner of Corunna Downs Station at that time. Later, Howden had married a white woman, and Nan became nursemaid to his daughter Judy. There were still quite close links between the Drake-Brockmans and our family. Nan and Judy were always friends, and I had asked Aunty Judy what she could tell me about the old days. But Howden had sold Corunna Downs when she was still quite small, and the family, together with Nan, had moved to a big house called Ivanhoe at Claremont, on the banks of the Swan River. So Judy Drake-Brockman was not able to tell me very much.

My mother did not really know who her father was, either. Nan had always refused to discuss the matter with her. Mum believed he may have been an Englishman, Jack Grime, who was a close friend of Howden Drake-Brockman, and lived at Ivanhoe.

During our visit to Corunna, we had discovered which tribal groups we belonged to. My mother, Gladys, was Panaka; I was Burungu; and Paul was Malinga. What had begun as a tentative search for knowledge grew into a spiritual and emotional pilgrimage. We now had an Aboriginal consciousness and were proud of it. By the time we left we had so much to think about, and much to come to terms with. And, as a result of what we had learned, we had more insight into Nan's bitterness, her refusal to talk about the past. More than anything we wanted her to change, to be proud of what she was. We had seen so much of her and ourselves in the wonderful people we'd met. We belonged to our Aboriginal heritage, now. We had found our place.

When we arrived back in Perth, Nan was really pleased to see us, and so was Beryl, a friend of Mum's who had been looking after her. Nan had gone through all the money Mum had left her and had had Beryl on the go non-stop, running up to the shop for chocolate biscuits and putting bets on the TAB.

We rounded up the rest of the family the following day and insisted on showing the video we had made of our trip. To our dismay, the film turned out to be pretty mediocre. It suffered from the faults common to most home movies: lack of focus, zooming too quickly and panning too slowly.

Throughout the filming of Corunna, I watched Nan. She was taking a keen interest in the old buildings.

'There's the old date palm,' she said. 'That used to be the garden down there. That's the old homestead, that part over there, that's where they had the kitchen.' When it was all over, she said, 'Fancy, all those old buildings still being there, I didn't think there'd be anything left.'

Mum told Nan what all the old boys had said about Lily, her and Arthur's full-blood half-sister. We had learned what a wonderful woman she had been, how caring towards the old people. Nan smiled. 'Ooh yes,' she chuckled, 'that was Lily, all right. She was the sort of person you couldn't help liking, she had a good heart, did Lily.' I was amazed. Nan had never talked like that before.

Over the next few days, Mum talked at length with Nan about the different people we had met. Nan feigned disinterest, but we knew it was just a bluff. She was desperately interested in everything we had to say, but she didn't want to let her feelings show. In many ways, she was a very private person.

One night, when they were alone, Mum told Nan how Annie, her mother, and a lot of the other older ones from Corunna Downs had died at Shaw River. 'She had Lily with her,' Mum said. 'Annie wasn't alone when she died, she had some of her people with her.'

Nan nodded. There were tears in her eyes. Her lips were set. 'Do any of them remember me?' she asked wistfully.

'They all do,' Mum said. 'They all remember you. Do you remember Topsy and another woman called Nancy? They said they lived with you and Annie on Corunna.'

'They still alive?' Nan asked in disbelief.

'Yes.'

Nan just shook her head. 'I'm going to bed,' she muttered.

Mum cried herself to sleep that night.

A few weeks later, I tackled Nan about being able to speak two languages. We had discovered that when Nan was at Corunna, she must have spoken two similar languages, Balgoo and Naml. I had once heard my Great-uncle Arthur and Nan speaking together in their own language, but Nan had been very annoyed about it. She was still unwilling to discuss the subject. She wouldn't be drawn further. There'd been a slight change, a softening, but she was still unwilling to share the personal details of her life with us.

'Do you reckon Jack Grime really is your father?' I asked Mum one day when we were alone together.

'Oh, I don't know, Sally.' Mum sighed.

'Aunty Judy said you're the image of Jack Grime. That'd be some sort of proof, wouldn't it?'

'Oh, I don't know, people can look like one another, but it doesn't have to mean they're related.'

'Hey, I know. I've got a photo of Jack, a big one, why don't we look at it, see if you do look alike?'

'I don't want to do that.'

'Go on! We'll hold it up to the big mirror in my room. You can put your head next to it and we'll see if you look like him.'

'Oh, all right,' Mum giggled, 'why not?'

Within minutes, Mum and I and the photo were all facing the large mirrors in the doors of my wardrobe.

'Well, that was a dead loss,' I said. 'You don't look anything like him. There's no resemblance at all.'

'He doesn't look like any of you kids, either, does he?'

'Naah,' I agreed. 'Hang on a tick, I'll get another picture.' I returned quickly. 'Okay,' I said, 'face the mirror.'

Mum fronted up to the mirror and tried not to laugh. She felt silly.

Suddenly, I held up a photograph of Howden as a young man next to her face. We both fell into silence.

'My God,' I whispered. 'He's the spitting image of you!'

Mum was shocked. 'I can't believe it,' she said. 'Why haven't I ever noticed this before? I've seen that picture hundreds of times.'

'I suppose it never occurred to you.'

'He couldn't be your father as well as Nan's. You know, features can skip a generation. Say he was Nan's father, well, you could have inherited those looks from that.'

'Oh, I don't know, Sally.' Mum sighed. 'It's such a puzzle. Nearly all my life, I've desperately wanted to know who my father was, but now, I couldn't care less. Why should I bother with whoever it was? They never bothered with me.'

'That's been the recent history of Aboriginal people all along, Mum. Kids running around, not knowing who fathered them. Those early pioneers, they've a lot to answer for.'

'Yes, I know, but I think now I'm better off without all that business. Those wonderful people up North, they all claimed me. Well, that's all I want. That's enough, you see. I don't want to belong to anyone else.'

'Me neither.'

We walked back to the lounge-room. After a few seconds'

silence Mum said, 'Sal...'

'What?'

'Aw...nothing. It doesn't matter.'

'I hate it when you do that. Come on, out with it.'

'We-ell...You know when we were at Corunna talking to old Jack, he told us he'd met someone called Daisy in 1923, a half-caste girl. He said she was pregnant. Do you think that could have been Nanna?'

'Dunno. I asked her the other day if she'd ever been back North, but she just got mad with me. But if it was her...Mum...do you think you might have a brother or sister somewhere?'

She nodded.

'But surely Nan would have told you?'

'Not if she wasn't allowed to keep it.'

'This is terrible.' I eyed her keenly. 'There's something you're not telling me, isn't there?'

Mum composed herself, then said: 'The other night when I was in bed, I had this sort of flashback to when I was little. I'd been pestering Nanna, asking her why I didn't have a brother or a sister, when she put her arms around me and whispered quietly, "You have a sister." Then she held me really tight. When she let me go, I saw she was crying.'

I couldn't say anything. We both sat in silence. Finally, Mum said, 'I'm going to ask her.'

A few days later, Mum broached the subject with Nan, only to be met with anger and abuse. Nan locked herself in her room, saying: 'Let the past be.'

'I'll never know now,' Mum told me later. 'She won't tell me.'

'You mustn't give up! What does your gut feeling tell you?'

'Oh Sally, you're like a detective. How do I know my gut feeling isn't pure imagination?'

'What does it tell you?' I persisted.

She sighed. 'It tells me I've got a sister. I've had that feeling all my life, from when I was very small, that I had a sister somewhere. If only I could find her.'

'Then I believe what you feel is true.'

Mum laughed. 'You're a romantic.'

'Be logical, she could still be alive, if she was born in 1923, she'd be in her sixties now. Also, if Nan had her up North, she could have been brought up by the people round there, or a white family could have adopted her.'

'Sally, you talk as though we'll find her one day, but it's impossible. We don't even have a name!'

'Nothing's impossible.'

'There's been so much sadness in my life,' Mum said, 'I don't think I can take any more.'

'You want to talk about it?' Mum had never told me everything about her early life. I knew that she had been sent to a children's home when she was little, but that was about all.

'You mean for your book?'

'Yes.'

'Well...' she hesitated for a moment. Then, with sudden determination, she said, 'Why shouldn't I? If I stay silent like Nanna, it's like saying everything's all right. People should know what it's been like for someone like me.' Then she said: 'Who knows? Perhaps my sister will read it.'

2
GLADYS CORUNNA'S STORY

(1931–1983)

Parkerville

I have no memory of being taken from my mother and placed in Parkerville Children's Home, but all my life I've carried a mental picture of a little fat kid about three or four years old. She's sitting on the verandah of Babyland Nursery, her nose is running and she's crying. I think that was me when they first took me there.

Parkerville was a beautiful place run by Church of England nuns. Set in the hills of the Darling Ranges, it was surrounded by bush and small streams. In spring, there were wildflowers of every colour and hundreds of varieties of birds. Each morning I awoke to hear kookaburras laughing and the maggies warbling.

Parkerville was my home from 1931, when I was three. I was only sent back to my mother at Ivanhoe three times a year, for the holidays.

There were two sections at the Home. The older children's section and Babyland Nursery. Babyland was really just a cottage surrounded by verandahs. Inside was a kitchen with a large wood stove, some small tables and chairs and high chairs for the really little ones. There was only one dormitory, filled with lots of little iron beds. They were very neat and tidy in Babyland. You were only allowed to play inside on real wintry days. Normally, they made us all sit out on the verandahs. That was so you didn't mess up the rooms once they'd been cleaned.

Every morning, the older girls came over to bathe us. We were always cold from the night before because we still all wet our beds. I dreaded bathtime because of the carbolic soap and the hard scrubbing brushes. The House Mother used to stand in the doorway and say, 'Scrub 'em clean, girls.' We'd cry, those brushes really hurt. Our crying always seemed to satisfy her, she'd leave then. As soon as she left, the girls would throw the brushes away and let us play.

Our clothes were kept in a big cupboard and the girls dressed us in whatever fitted.

I guess that was one of the few times when I was lucky to be black, because the older Aboriginal girls always gave us black babies an extra kiss and cuddle. You see, even though we weren't related, there were strong ties between us black kids. The older white girls never seemed to care about anyone, and our House Mothers weren't like real mothers, they just bossed us around, they never gave you a kiss or a cuddle.

Every morning, I'd sit on the verandah with my friend Iris. She had very white skin and her freckles stood out as though they'd been daubed on with a paintbrush. The older girls called her Chalky, because she was so pale. She always seemed to be unhappy, she had an awful cough and her feet were blue. We didn't have shoes. She loved to sit close to me. We'd play games with the toys that were scattered over the verandah. If we walked around, she liked to hold my hand. We always stuck together; if there were two of you, the others didn't pick on you so much.

After school, the older girls would come back and carry me around. When the bell rang, they'd all come running over, fighting about whose turn it was to carry me. I felt sorry for Iris then, no one ever wanted to carry her. I wished the big girls would play with her, too, but she was always coughing, and I was so busy enjoying the attention that I soon forgot her.

After tea, the girls would dress us in our night clothes, a one-piece suit with a square piece that buttoned at the back so we could go on the potty. The suit had feet, so they kept our toes warm.

Every little bed in the dormitory had a grey or dark-green blanket on it and we had to kneel down beside our beds to say our prayers. After that, the lights were turned out.

I remember one night hearing Iris cough and cough. I dozed off again and was awakened by the light being turned on and people walking in and out. When I got up in the morning, Iris was gone. I felt very lonely sitting on the verandah that day. I asked the others if they'd seen her. They said she was sick and had been taken to hospital. I felt very sad.

A few weeks after that, when I was playing on the verandah by myself, she just appeared out of nowhere. She was all dressed up in a white lace dress and she was happy, she wasn't coughing any more. She smiled at me and I smiled at her and then she left. I felt better then. I knew that wherever she'd gone, she was all right.

When I was five years old, I was sent to George Turner, the house opposite Babyland, across a wide expanse of gravel. I was told to go and see my new House Mother. I stumbled down the front steps and began walking across the gravel with my little bundle of clothes. I tried to walk on the clumps of dandelions to keep my feet clean, but they ran out when I reached the rainwater tank. After that, it was just black sand.

When I finally reached the gate of George Turner, I was too scared to open it. I was worried about my feet. In Babyland, it was very important that you kept your feet clean, that was why we were never allowed off the verandahs. Now here I was with black, sandy feet. I was sure my new House Mother would be cross with me.

Suddenly one of the older girls came up to the gate. I felt relieved when I recognised her, she was one of my friends. She took me by the hand and led me up to Miss Moore, who was waiting on the verandah.

Miss Moore showed me over the house. She said I was one of twenty-five children who would be staying here. She explained to me that the boys slept on one side of the verandah and the girls on the other, with a blind lowered in the middle to make a division. We each had a small cupboard for our own personal things and a small mirror so we could see to comb our hair in the mornings. I was amazed that she never once mentioned my dirty feet. I was also surprised to see that all the walls in the dormitories were covered with huge framed pictures. I was too young to know that they were pictures of film stars, I just thought they were pictures of Mummies and Daddies.

After Miss Moore had finished explaining things to me, she told me to put my things away. I never had much, just a few pieces of coloured Easter-egg paper and a one-legged teddy that I had hidden in my clothes and stolen from Babyland. All the way over, I had been worried that the teddy might fall out and they'd take it back. I was glad he was still with me. I also had a hairbrush that my mother had given me. She liked me to look neat.

My little cupboard wasn't bare for long, I became a hoarder. I loved collecting silver paper from Easter eggs. Sometimes, the big kids would give me some and I would sit for hours, trying to get the creases out. Then I'd stack them gently in an old chocolate-box. I collected anything the older children were willing to part with, I wasn't fussy. I loved hair-ribbons. Sometimes one of the older girls would help me get dressed and they'd tie a ribbon in my hair to make me look pretty. I'd show off to the kids who didn't have one.

I had nightmares at George Turner. I'd never had them in Babyland. I wasn't used to sleeping on the verandah. There were all sorts of noises that frightened me. The old canvas blinds would creak, the nightbirds called to one another; you often heard the wings of some large bird flapping past.

Sometimes, I'd wake in the night with a heavy weight on my chest and my mouth would be all dry inside. I was sure there was someone sitting on the end of my bed. I'd lie under the blankets, too scared to move or breathe. I thought, if I lay still enough, they might go away. I hoped that, because I was only little and didn't take up much room, they might think the bed was empty.

As I grew older, that fear disappeared. Maybe because I started to learn about Jesus. When I felt really scared, I'd look over the verandah to the tall gum tree nearby, and I'd see him there, watching me. I felt very protected. Sometimes, when I was sad, a light would shine suddenly inside of me and make me happy. I knew it was God.

Apart from these experiences, the thing that helped me most was the music I used to hear at night. As I grew older, I realised it was Aboriginal music, as though some blackfellas were having a corroboree just for me. After I'd heard it, I knew I could go to sleep. It gave me a feeling of protection.

I suppose it was healthy, sleeping on the verandah like that, but on wintry nights when there was lightning and thunder and the rain poured in, it was really scary. Of course, they pulled down the blinds all the way round to give us some shelter, but it was still frightening. I was sure one night I'd be struck by lightning.

There were many times when I felt very lost. I knew I wasn't a baby any more. I knew I had to look after myself, now.

One day, after I'd been at George Turner for about a year, some of the older girls asked me if I'd like to go for a walk. We walked deep into the bush on the far side of the Home. It was really lovely there. Sometimes, we'd disturb wallabies resting in the shade of the red gums. They'd hop a short distance away, they weren't upset by our presence, but their soft grey ears would twitch. They made sure we didn't get too close.

'Let's head for the cemetery,' one of the kids suggested.

'What's that?' I asked Enid, who was giving me a piggyback.

'It's where they put you when you die,' she replied. 'There's lots of babies buried there.' She'd been there often. Apparently, all the kids liked going there. They told me they liked to read the names printed on the crosses. Sometimes there'd only be a first name, like Rosie, with the age printed underneath.

Just as we were nearing the cemetery, I said to Enid, 'I thought you went to heaven with Jesus when you died.'

'You do,' she replied. 'We're here now, down you go.' She eased me off her back onto the ground.

I gazed at the little graves scattered here and there amongst the low clumps of red and pink bush. Then I followed Enid as she went from grave to grave, reading the names. Suddenly, she grabbed my hand.

'Look,' she said, 'see this one, it's that little friend of yours from Babyland — Iris, three years, ten months.'

I gazed in shock at the little mound of earth beneath the small white cross. Enid moved on, reading out the names of more babies as she went. I stood staring at Iris' grave. I suddenly realised that was why she hadn't come back to Babyland: she'd died.

I picked some buttercups and placed them on the top of the grave, the way I always did when I found a dead bird in the bush and buried it. I tried to hide my tears from the others, but they noticed and started chanting, 'Look at the sookie bubba!' Enid heard them and shouted, 'Leave her alone!' Then she ran back to me and picked me up. 'It's all right,' she said, 'your friend is happy in heaven.'

A Crying Tree

We had the same routine every morning at Parkerville. They woke us early by ringing a bell. The air was always cold and you never felt like getting up.

You made your bed, got dressed and swept down the verandahs. After that, it was time for breakfast.

During winter, we always had a big open fire going indoors, it got very cold in the hills. I remember, at night, we would hate leaving the fire to go out to our beds on the verandahs, they were so cold and draughty. I always tried to hide behind a chair, hoping Miss Moore wouldn't notice me. That way, I hoped I could huddle next to the fire all night. It was a trick that never worked, she always dragged me out and sent me off with the others.

Every morning, the boys got the wood for the stove in the kitchen and the older girls cooked the porridge. I never liked breakfast much. It was the weevils, they'd be there every morning, staring at me from my bowl of porridge. I covered them as much as I could with milk and sugar, and closed my eyes as they went into my mouth. I was always too hungry to allow myself to forgo the porridge. Apart from a slice of bread and dripping, the porridge was all we got.

After breakfast, we cleaned up, then went to morning church before school. At lunch-time, we all lined up and marched to the big dining-hall. Lunch was usually hot, often a stew. The meat sometimes smelt bad, especially in summer. After school, we were allowed one slice of bread and dripping before going to afternoon church. Tea was usually cold meat and salad and, if we were lucky, jelly and custard.

Every Friday night we had pictures, old silent movies, and we really loved them. Often, the films were quite heart-rending tales about gypsies stealing a child from a family. Of course, by the end of the film, they'd be reunited. I really identified with those films. We all did. I always thought of myself as the stolen child. In fact, I loved the part so whole-heartedly that it took me ages to come back to reality after the film had finished. We all loved any films about families. Pictures like that touched something deep inside us. It was every kid's secret wish to have his or her own family. But it was never something we talked about openly. During the week, we usually played the movies in our games. One of the most terrible punishments they could inflict on us was depriving us of our Friday night picture.

The first thing we did on Saturday mornings was line up for a dose of Epsom salts. It was revolting. After that, it was clean-up time. We washed the kitchen floor, wiped down the stove and cleaned out the bath with a mixture of charcoal and cooking salt. The job I hated most was cleaning the table we ate breakfast on. It showed every mark, we really had to scrub it to get it clean.

When it came to work, the boys had it real easy. The nuns considered looking after the house women's work. The boys never even helped with the floors. Though I didn't mind that, I loved polishing the floor. They gave us large tins of yellow polish which was made at the Home. We'd tie old woollen jumpers to our feet, slop huge lumps of wax on the floor, then zoom all over the place. It was better than roller-skating. We often banged into one another as well as the wall. Miss Moore only came in and checked on us if someone started crying. No matter how badly you hurt yourself, you never cried, otherwise everyone got punished. It didn't pay to upset Miss Moore, because she had a terrible temper and when she got angry, she could inflict terrible beatings.

After we'd finished the house, we'd all march over to the laundry to wash our clothes.

My favourite time at the Home was Saturday afternoons. Once we'd finished our work, we were allowed to do as we pleased. If it was too cold for swimming, we'd go hunting for food. I was always hungry. I was like Pooh Bear, I couldn't get enough to eat. My stomach used to rumble all the time. We loved to eat the wild cranberries that grew in the bush, they were sweet and juicy. Trouble was, the goannas liked them, too. You could be eating from one side, and a goanna from the other, and you never knew until you met in the middle. I don't know who got the biggest fright!

At the back of the dining-room was a shed used for storing apples and root vegetables. The door was always locked, but there was a small window we could easily climb through. We'd pinch some apples and potatoes then nick off into the bush to our special tree, where we liked to play Mothers and Fathers. It was a big, old red gum. It was dead and the trunk was split, so it was like a big room inside. It was a very happy place. We'd light a fire with a thick piece of glass we kept hidden. We'd shine it onto a dry gum leaf and, before long, the wisp of smoke would start to rise. We'd throw some more dry leaves on and get it going really good before we put the potatoes on. When we thought they were ready we'd haul them from the ashes by poking a long stick through them. Sometimes we'd burn our tongues, because our mouths would be watering too much to wait. Often the centre of the potatoes was raw, but we didn't care.

The best feed we had was gilgies. They were plentiful in the small pools and creeks around the Home. We caught them with a piece of old meat tied to a piece of string. When we'd caught nine or ten, we'd boil them up in an old tin.

Most of my happiest times were spent alone in the bush, watching the birds and animals. If you sat very quiet, they didn't notice you were there. There were rabbits, wallabies, goannas, lizards, even the tiny insects were interesting. I had such respect for their little lives that I'd feel terrible if I even trod on an ant. We'd come across all sorts of snakes, green ones, brown, black. Sometimes, the older boys used to kill the really big black snakes.

One day when I was on my own, I found some field mice under a rock near a honeysuckle vine. I often went to that vine, because the flowers were sweet to suck. It was almost as good as having a lolly. I thought the baby field mice were wonderful, they were pink and bald and very small. I decided it was a secret I'd keep to myself in case anyone harmed them.

As I sat looking at them, some boys suddenly appeared out of the bush nearby. When they saw what I was looking at, they ran over and pulled the mice out and held them high in the air, laughing and taunting me. They threw them to some kookaburras, who gobbled them up. I was really upset.

I had a crying tree in the bush. It was down near the creek, an old twisted peppermint tree. The limbs curved over to make a seat and its weeping leaves almost covered me. You didn't cry in front of anyone at the Home, it wasn't done. You had to find yourself a crying place. A lot of the kids cried in their beds every night, but it wasn't the same as having some place quiet to go where you could make as much noise as you liked.

I'd sit for hours under that peppermint tree, watching the water gurgle over the rocks and listening to the birds. After a while, the peace of that place would reach inside me and I wouldn't feel sad any more. Instead, I'd start counting the rainbow-coloured dragonflies that skimmed across the surface of the water. After that, I'd fall asleep. When I finally did walk back to the Home, I felt very content.

Saturday night was spent getting our clothes ready for church on Sunday. We ironed everything with those heavy flat irons you heated up on the stove. It was hard work, especially if you were little. Our clothes were always starched and ironed. We had to iron and iron until not one crease showed. It took ages.

I remember, one night, I went racing into the kitchen just as Miss Moore was coming through the door with a red-hot iron. It hit straight into my arm. I must have passed out, because when I woke up, I was in the Home Hospital with my arm all bandaged up and the Matron sitting beside me. They'd got the old doctor who serviced the Mundaring district to come and look at me. He only came to the Home in emergencies. They kept me in hospital four days. I was very lonely, no one else was sick. I think they felt sorry for me, because they let me sit out on the verandah with my arm in a sling. The other kids would sneak over and talk to me. The hospital was out of bounds, so they had to crawl through the big field of green peas opposite. I used to get cross with them because they took so long to crawl through that field. I knew they were all lying on their backs eating the peas, and had forgotten about me.

I was lucky that I didn't get ill too often. You didn't get on very well at Parkerville if you had something wrong with you and couldn't take care of yourself. All the weaker kids got stood over; the older kids picked on them. There were a lot of kids at the Home crippled with polio. I felt sorry for them. And you had to be dying not to go to school. If you stopped home, they gave you a dose of salts or castor oil. It cured everything in those days.

One of the lowest points of my childhood was the time they took me to Princess Margaret Hospital to remove my tonsils. I was so frightened. I was all alone and I thought I was going to die. I had to wear a nightie with the back all open. Everything smelt of carbolic soap, even the sheets. I hated that smell. They put me in a high iron bed and hardly anyone spoke to me. It was like being in a morgue. I was very sick after the operation and I cried and cried. I couldn't understand why my mother hadn't been to visit me, I thought perhaps they hadn't told her I was sick. She told me later that she couldn't get time off work and she couldn't come at night because of the curfew which prevented Aboriginal people travelling after dark.

It was hard for her then, and hard for me, too. Even when I was sick, I belonged to the Native Welfare Department. I wasn't even allowed to have the comfort of my own mother.

But just after this, something happened that really cheered me up. My Uncle Arthur visited. He'd come to see me once before at Parkerville when I was very small. The memory I had of him was only dim, but it was important. I loved him and I knew he loved me. I also knew that if he could have taken me from there, he would. He was very important to me. Sometimes, I used to think that if he and Mum could live together, then I'd have a family. It wasn't to be. He came and saw me once more after that, then never again. He was too busy trying to make a living for himself and his own family.

On Sunday afternoons, visitors were allowed to come. We used to wait and wait, we knew it was a long, uphill walk from the station, and we never knew whether someone was coming for us or not. That was the worst part. You hoped right up to the very last minute. I used to think, well, Mum will be here soon, I'll just wait a little bit longer. She'll be cross if she doesn't see me standing here, waiting for her. I remember some years when I only saw her twice at the Home. If no one came, you put on a brave face and didn't cry. You pretended you didn't care, you just shrugged your shoulders and walked away. If one of your friends got visitors, you'd be so jealous. Of course, if you saw someone coming over the hill for you, you'd get so excited you'd just run to them.

A lot of kids at Parkerville had parents. Some had mothers, some had fathers. You'd do anything for kids like that, because you always hoped that they might ask you to come along and share their visitors.

It was hardest for the Aboriginal kids. We didn't have anyone. Some of the kids there had been taken from families that lived hundreds of miles away. It was too far for anyone to come and see them. And anyway, Aboriginal people had to get permits to travel. Sometimes, they wouldn't give them a permit. They didn't care that they wanted to see their kids. Each time Mum came to see me, she always had a bit of paper with her that said she was allowed to travel. A policeman could stop her any time and ask to look at that paper. If she didn't have it on her, she was in big trouble.

When Mum didn't visit me for a long time, I used to wonder if she'd forgotten me. But the only day she had any time off was on Sunday, and then she had to cook the roast first. She never had any annual holidays, as some of the other servants did. And I remember quite a few times when she told me she hadn't come because she couldn't afford the train fare. The only time she had the whole Sunday off was if the Drake-Brockmans went visiting for the day.

When I was still quite young, Sister Kate* left Parkerville and took a lot of Aboriginal children with her. I was very sad, because I lost a lot of my friends. There were a few lightly

---

* *Sister Kate* — an Anglican nun who set up a Home for part-Aboriginal children in the 1930s. Initially, such children were sent to her by the Western Australian government authority responsible for Aborigines. Sister Kate's, as the institution became known, remains well-known today as a hostel and support organisation for Aboriginal children and families.

coloured Aboriginal boys left and they kept an eye on me. I don't know why I wasn't sent with Sister Kate, maybe it was because of the Drake-Brockmans, I don't know.

I think Mrs Drake-Brockman thought she was doing a good thing sending me to Parkerville. Sometimes, she'd come up and bring Judy, June and Dick with her for a picnic. That was always in spring, when the wildflowers were out. Dick and I got on well, we were very close. He treated me like his sister. I loved it when they all came up, because the other kids were so envious. There was a lot of status in knowing someone who had a car. I thought I'd burst for joy when I saw the black Chev creep up the hill and drive slowly down the road. All the other kids would crowd up close, hoping I'd take one of them with me. I'd jump down from the wooden fence we sat on while we waited and hoped for visitors and walk slowly towards the car. I felt very shy, but I was also conscious of the envy of the others still sitting on the fence behind me. It was a feeling of importance that would last me the whole of the following week. I always promised the other kids that next time, I might take one of them. It made me king until the following Sunday, when someone might get a visitor who brought a box of cakes. But cakes weren't as important as a car ride.

I often prayed to God to give me a family. I used to pretend I had a mother and a father and brothers and sisters. I pretended I lived in a big flash house like Ivanhoe and went to St Hilda's Girls' School, like Judy and June.

It was very important to me to have a father then. Whenever I asked Mum about my father, she'd just say, 'You don't want to know about him, he died when you were very small, but he loved you very much.' She sensed I needed to belong, but she didn't know about all the teasing I used to get because I didn't have a father, nor the comments that I used to hear about bad girls having babies. I knew it was connected to me, but I was too young to understand.

I had a large scar on my chest where my mother said my father had dropped his cigar ash. I tried to picture him nursing me, with a large cigar in his mouth. I always imagined him looking like a film star, like one of the pictures the big girls had. The scar made me feel I must have had a real father, after all. I'd look at it and feel quite pleased. It wasn't until I was older that I realised it was an initiation scar. My mother had given it to me for protection.

Treats And Punishments

We used to have quite a few outings at the Home. We went to the pictures and put on concerts at different places to raise money.

One morning, we were all very excited because we were going to the zoo. I really needed something to get excited about then, because I hadn't seen my mother for ages and I felt very sad. Actually, it wasn't only me. Hardly any of the kids had had visitors, they all felt down. There hadn't even been people looking for kids to adopt.

People often came to the Home to look kids over for adoption. I don't think they realised how upsetting it could be for everyone. We all got excited, we wondered who'd be the lucky one to get a Mother and a Father. The visits usually came to nothing, the kids would end up being turned down and they'd cry themselves to sleep.

A friend of mine did get adopted. Everyone was surprised, because usually, once you'd reached the age of eight or nine, no one wanted you. This girl was eight, she was very pretty with blonde hair. A wealthy family took her. We thought she was very lucky. She'd only been gone a couple of years when she died. There was a big court case about it. She died of arsenic poisoning. None of us wanted to be adopted after that.

Going to the zoo gave everyone a lift. After breakfast, we marched to the station. When the old steam engine came chugging in, we were all so frightened we'd be left behind that we ignored the screams of our House Mothers and jumped on while the train was still going. If you were first on, you always saved a seat for your mates and everyone hoped that their little group would end up in a carriage without a House Mother. That way, you could scream as loud as you liked when you went through the tunnel at Swanview.

The zoo was really exciting, especially the elephants. I'd seen pictures of elephants dressed up in gold, with Indian princes sitting on their backs. I could imagine myself doing that. I always remembered to smile at the elephants, because I'd read in a book that they never forgot, and there was a story about a man who was cruel to them so they'd trampled him to death. I believed in playing it safe.

I felt a lot happier after my day with the animals. We marched back to the ferry and were soon chugging back across the Swan River. I had a seat right up near the water and I watched as the ripples came out from under the boat and slowly faded away.

Then I noticed another ferry coming across from the other side, so I leaned over to look to see how close it would come to our boat. To my surprise, I saw my mother sitting on the ferry, as pretty as ever in her blue suit. I couldn't believe it. I called out to her, I shouted and waved my arms. She must have known I was going to the zoo, I thought, but she's got the wrong time, she's going to miss me. She might go to the zoo and I won't be there! I jumped up and down and called and called. My mother sat upright on the ferry, she never even turned her head in my direction.

Within minutes, our boats had passed, and I realised she hadn't heard me calling.

I slumped back on the wooden seat. The other kids just looked at me, they never said anything. I forgot all about the elephants and bears and lions. All I could think about was my mother. The sadness inside me was so great I couldn't even cry.

By the time I'd been in George Turner a couple of years, I began to get as adventurous as the other kids. I became a bit of a leader and had my own little gang.

Also, I wasn't scared at night any more. I actually came to love that part of the night when all the wild horses raced through. There were a lot of them in the hills in those days. When we heard them coming, we'd lean over the verandah and call out. They were so beautiful, some silver, some white, some black and brown. They were going down to the grassy paddocks on the other side of the hill. I suppose they were a bit like us kids in a way, they didn't belong to anyone.

There'd been a run of Tom Mix films on Friday nights and we'd all become interested in the Wild West. Sometimes, we'd pretend the Home's dunny cart was an old chuck wagon. We all had great imaginations.

Our enthusiasm for the Wild West led to a new interest in the wild brumbies. We decided that if we were really going to be like the cowboys, we needed a horse, so we thought we'd lasso one when they went through at night. But we had no rope. The only rope that we knew of was on the flag the school hoisted every Anzac Day. We knew where the flag was kept, so we drew sticks to see who would steal it. This was a practice we used to solve most of our problems. If you drew the long stick, you just accepted your fate, even though you were scared stiff.

Harry lost. Poor Harry, he was always getting into strife. It was just his luck. After he had sneaked over to the school and pinched the rope, we all leant over the verandah railings and waited in the dark for the horses to come through. We were very excited. Unfortunately, they always came through near midnight, so a lot of the smaller kids fell asleep over the verandah railings.

Round about eleven-thirty, we heard the rumble of hooves and knew they were on their way. Harry leapt onto the railings and got his lasso ready. When the brumbies came flying past, he flung the rope out as high and as far as he could, but when the rope disappeared, so did Harry. We watched in awe as he sailed over the railings, screaming. Once the horses had passed, we all ran down and found him lying in the dirt with his arm broken. We grabbed the rope and hid it, then went and woke Miss Moore.

'He was walking in his sleep,' we told her innocently, 'he fell off the verandah and broke his arm.'

That turned out to be a good excuse. We often used it after that when we were caught out of bed, playing dares.

I grew to love adventures, and I always knew I had to be brave, it didn't do to lose face in front of your friends.

There was an empty cottage where old Sister Fanny lived. Actually, she lived on part of the verandah, enclosed in hessian. It must have been very cold in winter. The inside of the cottage was used for visitors, who sometimes came and stayed overnight or for a few days. All the kids were too scared to go near Sister Fanny, we all thought she was a witch.

One day, some kids from a rival gang dared me to go right up to her. I wanted to back down, but, being a leader, I couldn't. Also, I'd been shooting my mouth off about how brave I was, so I had to live up to it.

I sneaked up very slowly to the cottage until I found myself standing just outside the hessian door that hung from the old tin roof. The flap swayed back and forth in the breeze and I could see inside to the dirt floor. There was a large black cat lying on the ground asleep. I was sure then Sister Fanny must be a witch; everyone knew witches had black cats.

I was so busy watching the cat, I didn't notice Sister Fanny. She pulled the hessian aside, stuck out her wrinkled face and said, 'Haaa!' I jumped back in shock. She had lank, uncombed shoulder-length hair and she looked very grubby. As I gazed at her face, I realised that she really did have one blue and one brown eye. The other kids had told me that, but I hadn't believed them.

'I just wanted to pat the cat,' I said quickly.

'Come in, child, come in,' she said in a thin, wobbly voice. I went inside and sat down and patted the cat. I thought if I patted it, it wouldn't hurt me.

Sister Fanny kept mumbling and walking around the room. I began to feel sorry for her, it was so shabby. There was an old iron bed and boxes for furniture, nothing nice. I realised then she wasn't a witch, just a frail old lady.

After a few minutes, I got up, said goodbye and rejoined the other kids. They couldn't believe I'd actually gone inside, they all thought I was really tough.

'You saw the witch,' they said, 'you saw the witch! What do you think, is she a real witch?'

'No,' I replied, 'and don't go throwing any more stones at her place. She's just an old lady.'

'Yeah, but she's got one brown eye and one blue,' said Tommy. 'Only witches have eyes like that!'

But I knew in my heart she was just an old lady.

There were a number of adults I became quite attached to and used to visit. I found I got on well with older people.

I regularly visited the office lady, Miss Button, to ask her if she had any jobs she needed doing. She was a particular friend of mine. She would get me to dust down her mantelpiece, then she'd make me a cup of tea and give me a biscuit. I was very excited when she went for a trip to England. She was always talking about England. Once, she'd shown me a map of the world and pointed out where England was. Just before she left on her trip, she promised me she'd send me a postcard. I couldn't believe it when it finally arrived. All the kids thought I must be really important to get a postcard from the country where the King and Queen lived. Next to God, they were the ones we stood in awe of.

About this same time, I was adopted by the Northam Country Women's Association as a needy child, and they decided that they would send me a gift at Christmas and on my birthday. A parcel arrived on my birthday, not long after Miss Button's card. I told all the kids that Northam was really in England and that my parcel had come from the King and Queen. I was lucky, because my present was a beautiful doll, and it looked English. It was the best birthday I ever had, even though the older kids said I was lying and that Northam wasn't in England.

While Miss Button was in England, I spent a lot of time visiting Miss Lindsay, another old girl who lived at the

Home. She had a tiny weatherboard cottage halfway between the last house and the hospital. She'd always been a part of Parkerville; no one could remember when she first came there. Whenever I visited her, I always took her a flower I'd pinched from the garden.

After Miss Lindsay had made a big fuss over my flower, she would go to her glass cabinet and take out a plate of small iced cakes. The first time I'd had a cake from Miss Lindsay, I'd taken a bite straight away and found, to my horror, that my fancy pink cake had cobwebs inside. I'd been really scared. Had I swallowed a spider? Would I die? I'd thanked her quickly, then rushed outside. For the next few days, I'd prayed that if I had swallowed a spider, it wasn't a poisonous one. By the end of the week, I was still alive, so I decided to start visiting Miss Lindsay again.

Now, being a little wiser, I was always hopeful, but ever cautious of her cakes. I never ate the cake in front of her. I'd just thank her then run out into the bush, where I'd carefully pull the cake apart before placing any of it in my mouth. I don't know why, but I kept going back, she kept giving me cakes, and they always had cobwebs in them. I hate to think how old they must have been. It was a long time before I gave up. I loved food so much.

At the opposite end of the Home to where Sister Fanny lived was the farm. Mr Pratt lived there, another of my favourite old people. He had a horse and buggy. The horse was called Timmy, he was big and black and beautiful. He was Mr Pratt's pride and joy; nobody else was allowed to ride him.

The old farmhouse was very tumbled down. Climbing roses had gone wild and covered most of the front yard, junk covered most of the back. Rusty machinery, tins, harnesses, old sheets of iron.

The older boys went over there regularly to milk the cows. We used to follow them. We'd lie back on the bales of straw in the milking shed and beg the boys to squirt us with milk. I had my mouth open all the time, it was lovely, feeling that warm, creamy milk shoot in and down your throat. It really warmed you up on a cold day.

Whenever Mr Pratt did the garden at George Turner, I'd follow him around, chatting about this and that. I liked talking to grown-ups and he was a darling old fellow.

One day, I was playing chasey with the others on the road, when someone yelled that I was wanted. I walked up the wooden steps onto the verandah. Little Faye was there, looking scared. 'Moore's in an awful temper,' she said, 'what have you done?' I mothered little Faye, and I knew she was worried about me.

'I'll be all right,' I replied. I patted her head and walked inside.

'Where's that Corunna kid?' I could hear Miss Moore screaming from the kitchen. What had I done? When I saw her, her face was contorted with rage. She grabbed me by the arm and started belting me across the head. It was nothing new, she'd given me beltings before. Sometimes, she hit me so much I'd go deaf for a couple of days.

She dragged me towards the large clothes cupboard. I started to cry, I didn't know what I'd done wrong. 'Get your clothes, you stupid girl,' she screamed. I was so upset, my eyes were too full of tears to see my clothes. Then she started shaking me and screaming that I had to be ready in fifteen minutes to go in the car. Where was I going? I felt very frightened. Were they sending me away? What about my mother, would I ever see her again? I started to tremble and shake all over.

I knew all the other kids would be outside listening to the goings-on. They kept out of reach when Miss Moore's temper was aroused. I tried to stop myself crying, but I couldn't, I started to sob.

I managed to get my clothes on, then splashed my face with cold water, but I still couldn't stop crying. Everything had happened so suddenly. Then I heard the car toot loudly out the front. Miss Moore hauled me out, picked up my bag of clothes and took me to the car. 'Stop snivelling,' she said, 'you didn't do anything wrong.'

I hopped in the front next to Willie, the driver, Sister Dora sat in the back. Willie started up the engine, then glanced down to me and said kindly, 'Don't cry any more, your mother will be all right.' I was really frightened then.

When we arrived at Ivanhoe, Alice Drake-Brockman took me to where my mother was lying in bed on the balcony. She looked terrible. Her eyes were closed and I thought she was dead. I tiptoed over and touched my mother's hand, resting on the white coverlet. She opened her eyes, tears trickled down her face, she squeezed my hand.

The following day, she told me what had happened. They'd taken my Aunty, Helen Bunda, to hospital, but her appendix had burst. They'd asked my mother to give blood. They'd taken the first lot, but it had jelled through carelessness, so they'd taken some more. 'They nearly killed me,' she whispered, 'I'll never go to hospital again.'

I asked her about Aunty Helen and she said,' Aunty Helen died. The doctor didn't care. You see, Gladdie, we're nothing, just nothing.'

I felt very sad, and sort of hopeless. I didn't want to be just nothing.

I stayed at Ivanhoe a week. When the others were asleep, I would sneak into bed with my mother. She'd cuddle me, silent tears wet on her cheeks. She seemed so unhappy that I'd cry, too, loving the comfort of her arms, yet sad at her tears.

I was upset that Aunty was dead, but I was glad Mum was getting better. Alice was very cross with the hospital. She made my mother eat to get her strength back. One day, when Mum was lying propped up on the pillows, someone from the *Daily News* arrived to take her photo. We were all very excited when we got the paper. Judy showed Mum her photo and read the article out to her. It said how she'd nearly sacrificed her life to save her cousin's and how brave she was. I felt very proud.

Everybody knew what had happened when I went back to Parkerville; some of the kids had seen my mother's picture in the paper. Miss Moore patted my shoulder and said she was pleased to see me back, but I couldn't look at her after the way she'd treated me. I felt betrayed.

Not long after that, I was playing in the garden when Mr Pratt rode by with the buggy and Timmy. I ran up to the fence and waved at him. He waved back. Suddenly, one of the wheels of the buggy caught in a rut in the road, the buggy overturned and poor Timmy fell and broke his leg. I screamed. There was Timmy, lying on his side in the dirt.

Mr Pratt gently undid the harness and talked to him in a loving way to keep him calm. Miss Moore came out and pulled me inside. She said I wasn't to go out until she said I could. Later, I heard the sound of a gunshot ring out and I knew Timmy was dead.

A few days afterwards, Mr Pratt was climbing a ladder at the farmhouse, when he suddenly fell to the ground, dead. I've always thought that the loss of Timmy was too much for him to bear.

Holidays

Easter was always a special time for me, I considered Good Friday the saddest day of the year. We'd attend church in the morning and after the service, we'd all file out solemnly. On the way back, we'd pass some of the graves of the early pioneers and that made Good Friday seem even more depressing. Once we were back at the house, we weren't allowed to play or make a noise.

Easter Sunday would change all that, we'd have a special midday dinner and an Easter egg. Kids who had relatives usually got visitors who brought more Easter eggs. My mother usually came to see me. It was a really happy day and I'd feel good because Jesus was alive again.

In the May holidays, I usually went to Ivanhoe. Willie would drive me down to Perth. I was always really excited that I was going to be with my mother for two whole weeks. She'd give me a hug then take me into the kitchen for a glass of milk and a piece of cake.

I loved Ivanhoe and I really loved Judy Drake-Brockman, she was so beautiful and she always made a fuss of me. She liked to dress me up, but I'd cry when she insisted on putting big satin bows in my hair. I didn't want to look like Shirley Temple.

I remember one holiday at Ivanhoe when I was very upset. I was in the kitchen with my mother. She had her usual white apron on and was bustling around when Mrs Drake-Brockman came in with June, who had the most beautiful doll in her arms. It had golden hair and blue eyes and was dressed in satin and lace, like a princess. I was so envious, I wished it was mine.

June said to me, 'You've got a doll, too.' Then, from behind her back, her mother pulled out a black topsy doll dressed like a servant. It had a red checked dress on and a white apron, just like Mum's. It had what they used to call a slave cap on its head, really just a handkerchief knotted at each corner. My mother always wore one on washing days, because the laundry got very damp with all the steam and the cap stopped it trickling down her face.

I stared at this doll for a minute. I was completely stunned. *That's me*, I thought. But I wanted to be a princess, not a servant. I was so upset that when Judy's mother placed the black doll in my arms, I couldn't help flinging it to the floor and screaming, 'I don't want a black doll, I don't want a black doll!' Mrs Drake-Brockman just laughed, but I clung to my mother's legs and cried and cried. She growled at me for being silly and bad-mannered in front of Mrs Drake-Brockman, but I knew she didn't really mean it. I could hear the sadness in her voice. She understood why I was upset.

They told the story of this often at Ivanhoe. They thought it was funny. I still can't laugh about it.

It was terrible in the 1930s, during the Depression. People were so poor, especially Aboriginal people.

They would come along the river, selling clothes-props,

long, wooden poles people used to prop up their clotheslines. I think they liked calling at Ivanhoe, because my mother was allowed to give them a cup of tea and a piece of cake or bread. I used to feel so sorry for these Aboriginal people. They had nothing, especially the old ones. Many of them had been separated from their kids and they had no one to look out for them.

My mother loved it when they came, she'd sit on the lawn with them and they'd talk about how it used to be in the old days. My mother always gave them clothes and shoes, whatever she could find. When they left, she'd have tears in her eyes. It hurt her to see her own people living like that.

At Christmas, I also went to Ivanhoe. We'd all sleep out on the balcony at the rear of the house, with a lovely view over the Swan River.

At the top of the house was a large attic which June was allowed to use as a playhouse. There were seats under the windows, dolls and a dolls' house, teddies and other toys and a china tea-set. We'd play tea-parties. June's china dolls were lovely.

At the Home, nobody owned a doll. There were a few broken ones kept in the cupboard, but when you asked to play with them, you had to play in the dining-room. You were never allowed to take one to bed. I was lucky, because I had a rag doll my mother had given me called Sally Jane. I loved her very much. She was kept at Ivanhoe for me and Mum let me take her to bed every night.

On Christmas morning, we'd wake up early and check the pillowslips we'd hung on the ends of our beds the night before. Judy's mother always gave me a new dress, with hair ribbons to match. Mother always made me doll's clothes and I would dress Sally Jane in one of her new dresses. We were very happy together, Judy, June, Dick and I. It was like having a family.

Every year after each of the holidays, I found it harder and harder to leave my mother and return to Parkerville. I couldn't understand why I couldn't live at Ivanhoe and go to school with Judy and June. You see, I hadn't really worked out how things were when your mother was a servant. I knew the family liked me, I just couldn't understand why they didn't want me living there.

School

At school I used to gaze out of the window a lot. And I was always getting into trouble. It wasn't that I was a cheeky child, it was just that everybody got into trouble, in those days. Usually, I managed to get out of it by making up a good story; there were only a few occasions when I wasn't quick enough to think up something convincing. I think one of the reasons I survived was because I learnt to lie so well.

You see, if there was an argument or if something had been damaged, and it was your word against a white kid, you were never believed. They expected black kids to be in the wrong. We learnt it was better not to tell the truth, it only led to more trouble. The Home also taught us never to talk openly about being Aboriginal. It was something we were made to feel ashamed of.

One year, we had a school play that was a great success. It was shown to people from the surrounding districts and was greeted with great enthusiasm. I was chosen to play the part of the fairy princess.

Actually, it was lucky I was chosen to do anything, because the year before, I'd disgraced myself in public. I was in the choir and had quite a good voice, so they decided I could sing a solo. When we gave our first public concert, I just looked at all those strange faces and froze. I opened my mouth, but nothing came out. Sister Dora, who was head nun at Parkerville, had been really embarrassed.

Sister Rosemary had chosen me to play the part of the fairy princess, and when Sister Dora objected, she said there was nothing to worry about, because I didn't have to say anything. I had to wear a long, flowing gown with a jewelled crown on my head, walk to the centre of the stage, then back to my throne while all the elves paid homage to me. I loved it. I decided that when I grew up I would be a film star.

The play was so popular that the Home decided to put it on in a hall next to Christ Church Grammar in Claremont. We were all loaded onto a big cattle truck and off we went. The play went well, with lots of loud applause at the end. I was very proud, because all the Drake-Brockmans were in the audience and, more importantly, so was my mother. When it was all over, I only had a moment for a quick hug before being loaded back onto the cattle truck and taken home again.

When I was about eleven, we got a new headmaster at Parkerville, Mr Edwards. He was different to the old headmaster, he didn't yell so much. He encouraged my interest in poetry and introduced me to algebra. I loved both those things. When he realised that I'd read all the poetry books in the library and knew many poems off by heart, he lent me some of his own books, including a set of Shakespeare's plays. I read all of them and loved every one. I suddenly found that school didn't have to be dull after all, it could be quite exciting. I was no longer a middle-of-the-class student, I progressed to the top.

Even though I was older now, I was still getting into scrapes. We'd go out in our little gangs and steal fruit from the surrounding orchards. I'll never forget one Sunday night, Mr Tindale, the minister, was preaching his usual hellfire-and-brimstone sermon, when he suddenly stopped and pointed to the congregation. Then he said in a loud thundery voice, 'Whoever has been stealing apricots from the Johnson farm will go to hell! I want the gang who did it to come and see me tomorrow afternoon after school. If you take your punishment, there might be some hope for you.'

He continued to rant and rave about the devil and bang his fist on the pulpit. Mr Tindale always wore long, flowing, black robes, so I could imagine just what the devil looked like.

Sister Dora loved his sermons, she would almost stand in

her seat when he shouted that we were all going to hell and her eyes lit up whenever he mentioned the devil.

Anyhow, this time I was really scared, because I felt sure he knew it was my gang that had been raiding the Johnson farm. What could I do? I hated being caned. I'd managed to talk my way out of trouble a lot in the past, and I wondered what kind of story I could invent to get out of this one.

As we were filing out of church, Margaret, a girl from another gang, whispered to me, 'How did he find out?'

'Dunno.'

'I was sure no one had seen us pinch that fruit,' she said. 'Guess we'll just have to face the music now.'

'Were your lot stealing apricots from there?' I asked.

'Yeah. And I'm not looking forward to the stick,' Margaret grimaced.

I felt very close to her at that moment. I also felt very guilty. To compensate, I gave her half the chewing-gum from my mouth. She was very pleased; gum was hard to get.

One day, we were banned from going to a certain part of the bush. The rumour was that a boy had hanged himself there. The House Mothers said it wasn't true, but I think it was. They said the boy had been sent somewhere else. It made me feel very sad. I never went to that tree again. I think it could have happened, because unless you could look out for yourself, you had a bad time. You could feel so low that you'd want to die.

Towards the end of the school year, we'd be given our annual outing to the pictures. We went by train to Perth, then marched up Plaza Arcade to the Royal Theatre in Hay Street.

The other Homes would be there, too, Sister Kate's and Swanleigh. Some of the kids would be very excited, because they had brothers and sisters in the other Homes and it was the only time of the year they saw them. I used to feel glad then that I was an only child, it always upset me to think that all they saw of the rest of their family was just a glimpse and a wave before we were all ushered into the theatre.

As we moved through the theatre doors, we were handed

a paper bag containing sandwiches, a cake and lollies. It was such a treat. I always tried to sit upstairs or under the balcony, but never in any other part of the theatre, because you got pelted with bits of leftover food. The yelling and screaming had to be heard to be believed, there was absolutely no control. The House Mothers tried, but there wasn't any point in them shouting at us, because we couldn't hear them. It was one of the best days in the year.

Change Of Scene

I didn't go to Ivanhoe that Christmas because they had other people staying there. I couldn't understand this, I didn't take up much room. Sister Rosemary had tears in her eyes because I was so upset. 'Never mind, dear,' she said, 'you'll be going to the beach.' It was no consolation. I felt really hurt, it seemed as though no one wanted me.

The Home had a large, rambling house at Cottesloe that was used for holidays for children who had nowhere else to go. Each child was allowed to stay for two weeks. We went by train to Perth, then changed trains for Cottesloe, it was the longest train ride I'd ever had.

The house was so close to the beach it took only a few minutes to walk down. Every room was filled with beds so as many children as possible could fit in. The dining-room was packed with wooden tables and benches. We had plenty of food, and the kitchen staff let us help ourselves whenever we felt hungry.

By this time, I had made friends with a girl called Margot. She was a few years older than me and very pretty. One day, we were racing into the waves and laughing, when two boys came and joined us. I was completely tongue-tied, I couldn't think of a thing to say. Margot, full of confidence, spun them a story about us being on holiday from the country. You never told anyone you were from a Home, because people seemed to look on you as some kind of criminal.

When the other girls found out that we were seeing two

boys, they looked at me through new eyes. I wasn't just a kid any more. That night, I spent ages admiring myself in the bathroom mirror. I could see only my head and shoulders in my mirror at George Turner, so it was really wonderful to be able to look into this full-length one and see the whole of me. I was really surprised, because my figure had changed. I was taller and my stomach had almost disappeared. I'd carried it around with me for so long I wondered how it could have gone without me noticing it. My hair was a bit longer and it was black and curly. I realised suddenly that I really was pretty, people weren't just being polite saying that. I felt more confident, seeing myself in this new light, but I stopped going to the beach with Margot. I wasn't keen on seeing those boys again.

I felt different after coming back from Cottesloe in the new year. Even Miss Moore treated me as an older girl, now. I was allowed to stay up for an extra half-hour after the little ones had gone to bed. Miss Moore let me read some of her magazines and she'd bring in her wireless and we'd listen to the news.

When I went out to bed, I'd tuck little Faye in, it was a habit I'd got into over the years. I felt really sorry for the little ones at George Turner, and I had never forgotten how sad I'd been when I left Babyland. They often needed comforting at night. They'd turn their faces into the pillow and cry, because they knew if Miss Moore heard them, she'd give them a smack. She hated being disturbed at night.

I couldn't stand it if they cried too long, I'd take them into bed with me. Sometimes when they cried, they wet their beds, and they were terrified of getting into trouble about it. I'd get up and change their beds and hide their wet sheets and pyjamas in the bottom of the laundry basket. They always wanted me to be their mother. I felt guilty because sometimes, I used to get sick of them.

One of my favourite jobs was going over to Babyland and looking after the very little ones. My friend Pat had a little sister there. There were four kids from her family at Parkerville and the terrible thing was they were all put in different houses. Pat's baby sister thought I was her mother. I used to cry for all those little kids. They had no one.

Even though I was twelve now, no one had told me the facts of life. We were totally ignorant about the things that could happen to our bodies. The older girls never told you anything, they'd just laugh and keep everything a secret. We were all so innocent it would have been easy for someone to take us for a ride. We had no protection. There must have been cases of kids being molested; I was lucky, it never happened to me. No one would believe you if you complained about things anyway — adults were always right, kids had no say.

I was also aware that I was changing, growing up, because boys I had previously fought with now seemed embarrassed in my company. The old easygoing atmosphere had gone. I guess they were changing, too.

One Sunday, my mother visited. I could tell she was upset as soon as I saw her. We went for a walk and she told me that Alice Drake-Brockman had asked her to leave Ivanhoe. 'She said she can't afford to keep me any more,' she said bitterly. 'All the years I've been working for that family and they can't afford to keep me!'

She was very hurt. I was confused; I had felt like part of the family and now Mum was no longer going to have anything to do with them. I felt very unsure of myself.

It was well known around Claremont what a good worker my mother was. I think people felt sorry for her for the way she'd been treated. A Mrs Morgan offered Mum a job as a live-in housekeeper and she said that I would be allowed to go and stay there on holidays. Mum was only too pleased to accept this offer. It was the first time she'd been out on her own in the world. She had always told me that she'd be at Ivanhoe for ever, that it was her home. The Morgans were good to Mum. They gave her an increase in pay, she had a nice room and, for the first time in her life, annual holidays.

Going to Morgans' was the best thing that could have happened to her, she developed a new independence. It was a different atmosphere, they'd never had a servant before. They didn't have old-fashioned attitudes towards her. Also, this new job was a proper business arrangement.

I loved it when she was there, it meant she could come to the Home and spend her annual holidays with me. The nuns let her sleep in a room just off one of the school buildings and they let me sleep there, too. A couple of times, she brought the two Morgan girls, June and Dianna, up with her. They were nice girls and enjoyed all the bush around the Home.

In the morning, we'd walk down to the grocer's at the bottom of the hill. There was a deep creek that ran past the store, spanned by a wooden bridge. I could never take my eyes off the jars of lollies of all sizes and colours. Hard-boiled striped candy-sticks stood on the front counter, next to large tins of mixed biscuits. Mum would buy me a bag of chocolate biscuits — she knew they were my favourites.

I was very popular with the other children at this time. I felt sorry for them, they all wanted mothers, too. They'd rush over when we were sitting on the lawn and would want to sit near my mother and touch her, especially the little ones. She always gave them a lolly, but I think it was when she spoke to them or kissed them that they were really happy. That was what they really wanted. She was a very kind person and tried to make a fuss of everyone.

At Christmas, I went and stayed at Morgans'. Although I missed Ivanhoe, I liked June and Dianna, and Mum now had more time for me, because there was less work to do. I was pleased for her; I was sick of seeing her work so hard.

After Mum had been at Morgans' about two years, the Drake-Brockmans asked her if she would come back to Ivanhoe to work. I wanted her to stay at Morgans', because it was easier for her, but I think Mum still felt a loyalty to the family. It was easy for people to make her feel sorry for them. She was too kind-hearted. Mrs Drake-Brockman's mother had come to live with them and she was very difficult to look after. I think that's why they wanted Mum back. She had to accept a cut in wages and no annual holidays, but she went anyway. She told me that it was to be permanent, she'd never be leaving there again.

I went to Ivanhoe for Christmas that year — I was about fourteen by then. Judy, June and Dick suddenly seemed a lot older than me. It wasn't the same as our carefree childhood days. Even though we had all loved each other as children, something had changed. Judy, June and Dick had begun to get more like their mother. They treated Mum like a servant now, she wasn't their beloved nanny any more.

June had a friend who was a bit of a snob and this girl was always putting me in my place because I was only the maid's daughter. I'd go and sit in Mum's room and cry. I was suddenly very unsure of my place in the world. I still ate with the family in the dining-room, but I felt like an outsider, especially when Alice would ring a little brass bell and my mother would come in and wait on us.

I suddenly realised that there hadn't been one Christmas dinner when Mum had eaten her meal with us. She'd had hers alone in the kitchen all these years. I never wanted to be in the dining-room again after that, I wanted to be in the kitchen with my mother.

After the summer holidays, Mum took me back to Parkerville, but when I got there, I discovered that Miss Moore had left and I was to have a new House Mother. I felt terrible, I had been living with Miss Moore for nine years and I hadn't even had the opportunity to say goodbye to her.

Why was everything changing? My new House Mother had been an enemy of Miss Moore's and I knew she'd take it out on me. Even though Miss Moore had belted me a lot, I was considered one of her pets. I just knew I'd have a bad time.

Also, I was worried that I'd get sent out to work as a domestic and never see my mother again. All the Aboriginal girls were sent out as domestics once they reached fourteen. Only the white kids were trained for anything.

I cried and cried and begged Mum not to leave me there.

I was so upset I went to the office with Mum to see Sister Dora and Miss Button. I had to sit on a wooden bench outside and wait while Mum went in.

Finally, they called me in, and Miss Button said, 'Do you want to leave here, Gladys? Your mother has said she wants to take you with her.' She smiled kindly at me.

'Oh yes,' I replied, 'yes, please!' I couldn't believe it, to be with my mother for always, it was too good to be true. I walked over to George Turner to pack.

Pretty soon, the news spread that I was leaving. All the kids crowded round and I handed out keepsakes from my locker. As we set off down the hill, I waved goodbye. I was very excited to think that at last, Mum and I were going to live at Ivanhoe together. Maybe my childhood dream would come true and I'd be the same as Judy and June. Maybe we'd be one big, happy family, after all. That was what I wanted more than anything.

Claremont

It wasn't long before my dreams came crashing around my feet. Alice Drake-Brockman was very cross with Mum for bringing me back. She said I couldn't live at Ivanhoe, I wasn't wanted.

It took a week for Mum to find a family who would take me in. The Hewitts had three boys and often took in older girls. I got on well with the boys and enrolled in Claremont High School. I tried not to think about Ivanhoe. I wasn't allowed to stay there weekends, either. If Mum wanted to see me, she had to visit at the Hewitts'. I felt very hurt by it all.

The Hewitts were very religious. I'll never forget the first Sunday morning they took us all down to Fremantle. I thought we were going to church, I never realised they intended holding a revivalist meeting on a street corner.

We all stood around in a circle and Mr Hewitt handed me a hymn book. Everyone started singing loudly, raising their hands and shouting, 'Praise the Lord!' As the meeting got more exuberant, one or two would suddenly leap into the air, shouting, 'Hallelujah brother, Praise the Lord!'

A lot of people started gathering round and I slowly moved backwards into the crowd, lowering my hymn book as I went. I thought I'd try to pretend I was one of the onlookers. Unfortunately, Mr Hewitt, who was really quite a sweetie, noticed what I was doing. He grabbed me by the arm and drew me back into the wild circle of worshippers. He whispered in my ear, 'Sing, Glad, sing. Raise your voice to heaven!'

We'd all sing loudly, more people would leap into the air, shouting, 'Hallelujah!' then we all had to echo it. The meeting got more and more frenzied and the minister started shouting out to the onlookers: 'Repent before it's too late!' All the sinners gathered round seemed quite impressed with the whole proceedings. I suddenly felt a dig in my back and a voice said, 'Now!' I found myself suddenly yanked from the circle and pulled away. I was amazed when I saw that my rescuer was Warren, the Hewitts' eldest son. We made our way through the entranced crowd and stood against a shop wall.

'I saw you trying to hide before,' said Warren. 'Isn't it embarrassing?'

'Yes,' I groaned. 'I had no idea it would be like this. I thought we were going to church.'

'We do this every Sunday, you have to be dying to get out of it.'

'Oh, no,' I sighed. 'I hope no one I know ever sees me!'

I had been worrying about starting Claremont High School. I didn't want anybody to find out I'd been in a Home and I was concerned that I wouldn't be able to make friends.

As it turned out, I got along with all the other kids really well, especially Noreen and Doreen, who became my very best friends. Noreen was Scottish and was only in Australia because of the war. It was 1940, and she had been sent out with a lot of other children for safe-keeping. She had a terrific sense of humour. I spent a lot of time at her house.

Every lunch hour at school, we had air-raid drill. There was a park nearby, with trenches dug in case we were ever bombed. At lunch-time, they'd blow the siren and we all had to run as fast as we could and jump in the trenches. You can imagine the shambles there was, we'd all leap in and fling up sand at each other. It was chaos.

In one way the war really affected our education. All the young men had joined up and I suppose some of the women had been manpowered, so all our teachers were really old.

I'll never forget Miss Edwards. Her fiancé had been killed in World War One and she was very sentimental. She loved reading us romantic novels, especially *Wuthering Heights*. She would sit out the front of the class with tears streaming down her face. Now and then, she'd have to stop completely and blow her nose and try and pull herself together.

During our lunch hour, Noreen, Doreen and I would walk down to the Claremont Shopping Centre. I was always the last back, so I'd call in to the florist and ask if there were any leftover flowers that I could give an old lady who was sick. They always managed to scrounge me up a few and I'd present them to Miss Edwards when I got back to school. There'd be tears in her eyes.

One day, I was so tired that I went to sleep in class and Miss Edwards noticed. 'I think you'd better sit outside for a while, Gladys,' she said, 'the fresh air might wake you up.'

I was really scared. I knew that if Mr Simms, the headmaster, came along and saw me sitting there, he'd know I had done something wrong. I nearly died when I saw the Head coming down the hall. I sat with my head bowed, hoping that he wouldn't notice me. I couldn't bear to think of being caned.

He stopped when he got to me and said, 'What are you doing out here, girlie?'

I peered up at him. He was a tall, plump man, with small round specs perched on the end of his nose.

'I feel sick,' I said, which was the truth.

'You poor child,' he murmured, 'you shouldn't be sitting out here. Come into the office.' I followed him down the hall into his office.

'Now, girlie,' he said, 'have you eaten lunch? I know what you young people are like, you get talking and playing and you forget to eat your lunch.'

I thought of all the fabulous biscuits and cakes that the teachers had for morning tea, so I couldn't help replying, 'I haven't eaten anything.'

'I thought so,' he said. 'No wonder you feel sick.' He sat me down at his desk and deposited a large glass of milk in front of me, a plate of iced cakes and a huge tin of cream biscuits. 'Eat!' he commanded.

I didn't need to be told twice.

'I have to go,' he said, 'but when you've finished, lie down on that old cane lounge, and when the bell goes, you can go home.'

About an hour later, the bell woke me and I got up and left. As I was walking down the hall, Miss Edwards saw me and called, 'Gladys, where did you get to?'

'Mr Simms took me into his office,' I told her.

'Serves you right, Gladys,' she said. 'I don't mind you being late, but you must never go to sleep when I'm reading Jane Austen.'

It was during that year in high school that Mum left Ivanhoe again. I was really angry about that. She'd given up a good job to go back and now she was told that they didn't need her any more and she'd have to find somewhere else to live.

Mum was very hurt. She had pay owing to her which I don't think she ever got. I was glad now that I didn't belong to them.

One of Mum's friends told her about a cook's job in the Colourpatch restaurant, a little place just opposite the Ocean Beach Hotel, which was an R and R place for American sailors. There were lots of American sailors there during the war.

Most of the help in the restaurant was voluntary, but the cook's job was a paying one. Mum applied for the job and got it.

Molly Skinner, the author, owned a house just behind the

hotel and she said Mum could pay rent and live with her if she wanted to. Molly was very sympathetic to Aboriginal people. Mum moved in with her. Molly also said that I could come and stay on weekends. I was very pleased about that, because I had hardly seen Mum for the past few months.

I think Mum would have liked me to live with her fulltime, but she lacked the confidence to move me away from the Hewitts'. She was frightened that something might go wrong and I'd be taken away. She knew Aboriginal people like her weren't allowed to have families.

I loved spending weekends with her, she'd spoil me, and Molly Skinner was always pleased to see me. Every Saturday afternoon, Mum would give me threepence to go to the pictures with Noreen and Doreen. We had great fun. All the kids from school would be there and we'd yell and scream.

The Colourpatch was really busy on Sundays, so Mum often got me to help out with the waitressing. The Americans were lovely, they'd leave large tips for me under their plates. All the other waitresses had to hand their tips in, but I was allowed to keep mine. I think it was because Mum was such a good cook. She always gave everyone double helpings and nothing was too much trouble for her. I think she felt sorry for a lot of the servicemen there; some of them were only boys. It was a really happy time for me.

One Sunday night, I arrived back at the Hewitts' to be met with serious faces from the whole family. Mrs Hewitt took Mum into the lounge and I had to sit in the hall.

'You're in big trouble,' Warren whispered. I didn't know what I'd done wrong. Then the youngest Hewitt boy came out and said, 'Gladys, you've sinned!'

A few minutes later, Mrs Hewitt came out and said, 'Will you please come in, Gladys?'

I looked at Mum. She was sitting in a chair beside the open fireplace. She looked completely dumbfounded.

'Now, Gladys,' said Mrs Hewitt, 'I am going to ask you a question and I want you to answer truthfully. Did you go to the pictures, did you enter that house of sin on Saturday afternoon?' I couldn't think of what to say. 'It's no use trying to deny it,' she said. 'One of the ladies from the church saw you.'

That was when I hung my head. I didn't feel sinful, I'd had a great time, but I felt it was expected of me. Mrs Hewitt turned to Mum and said, 'I don't think it will be suitable for Gladys to stay here any longer. I'm trying to turn her into a good Christian and you're letting her sin on Saturday afternoons!'

Mum just looked at me. She'd never heard of pictures being sinful before.

Mrs Hewitt pointed to the corner of the room and said, 'Gladys, I've taken the liberty of packing your suitcases, I think you'd better go now.'

Mum and I went back to Cottesloe. We didn't know what to say to each other. For the first time in our lives, we were together. I don't think Mum knew how to handle it. She was too scared to realise that it had actually happened. She was my mother and I was her daughter and we could be a family now. I think she was afraid to get used to it in case I got taken away from her again.

Miss Skinner was very happy to have me at her house.

'I'm Aboriginal'

I finished school at the end of 1943. I was sixteen. All my friends were going on to business college, but I knew that wasn't possible for me.

I spent my time helping Mum in the restaurant. I was put in charge of milkshakes in the lolly shop attached to the Colourpatch. I took great pride in my work. People would come from miles to buy a milkshake from me. I experimented all the time and would put in great dollops of ice-cream. They took me off the milkshakes eventually, I don't think they made any profit.

After a while, Alice Drake-Brockman got me a job on trial with a florist in Claremont at six shillings a week. It was a funny set-up in those days. If you were monied people or if you had a name, like Drake-Brockman, it was 'Open Sesame'. People ran after you, they rushed to serve you. There are some people who still do it today.

I was very excited about my job. I used to ride from Cottesloe to Claremont on an old bike.

Kathy, the other junior who worked there, was great. She was as fair as I was dark. She warned me about my new boss, Mrs Sales. 'She's a bit of an old cow,' she said. 'She'll leave money on the floor just to see if you'll pinch it, so watch out.'

Sure enough, I was told to sweep the shop and there, on the black oiled floor, was a two-shilling piece. I gave it to the boss, she feigned surprise and put it in the till. A week later, there was another two-shilling piece on the floor. I handed that in, too, and that was when I was told that from then on, I was on staff and would get ten shillings a week.

Mrs Sales had another florist shop on the corner of Broadway. I used to catch the trolley bus down and take flowers for them to sell. The junior there was called Violet, she was a nice girl and we became friends.

Kathy, Violet and I were all about the same age. We got plenty of attention from the Americans, because they were always going into florist shops to order corsages for their girlfriends. They were very different to Australian men, much more polite.

About a year later, Kathy became engaged to an American sailor, so we'd often go to the pictures with his friends. I had a great time until they got serious; Americans always wanted to get engaged. For the first time in my life, I felt free. I didn't have to answer for everything I did. Of course, Mum tried to be very strict with me. Even though it was all very innocent she was so suspicious. She kept saying I didn't know what the world was like or what men were like. I realise now that she was right. I had had a very protected life.

It wasn't long before I'd become very good friends with one of the customers, an English lady called Lois, and it was through Lois that I met a nice Scottish sailor. I went out with him for quite a while; it was a good friendship. For once,

Mum approved. She knew how wild the Yanks were, so I suppose she thought I'd be safe with a Scotsman.

Every weekend, the Yanks had a wild brawl down on the seafront and the police were called in. It was almost a regular outing for them. It was difficult during the war, some of the men had been through terrible things. I think they needed to let off steam some way.

I remember, one Sunday, I was waiting at a bus stop, when a lady came along. We started to chat.

'You're very beautiful, dear,' she said. 'What nationality are you, Indian?'

I smiled. 'No. I'm Aboriginal.'

She looked at me in shock. 'You can't be,' she said.

'I am.'

'Oh, you poor thing,' she said, putting her arm around me, 'what on earth are you going to do?'

I didn't know what to say. She looked at me with such pity, I felt really embarrassed. I wondered what was wrong with being Aboriginal. I wondered what she expected me to do about it.

I talked to Mum about it and she said I must never tell anyone what I was. She made me really frightened. I think that was when I started wishing I was something different. It was harder for Mum than me because she was so broad-featured she couldn't pass for anything else. I started noticing that when I went out with her, people stared at her. I hadn't realised that before.

The conversation with that lady at the bus stop really confused me. Suddenly I felt like a criminal. I couldn't understand why I felt so terrible. Looking back now, I suppose she knew more about how Aboriginal people were treated than I did. She probably knew I had no future, that I'd never be accepted, never be allowed to achieve anything.

For a while after that I tried to talk to Mum and get her to explain things to me, especially about the past and where she'd come from. It was hopeless, we'd been apart too long to get really close. I knew she loved me and I loved her, but all through my childhood, she had been just a person I saw on holidays. She just kept saying, 'Terrible things will happen to you if you tell people what you are.' For her sake as well as my own, I thought I'd better keep quiet. I was really scared of authority. I wasn't sure what could happen to me.

Then Molly Skinner sold her house, so we had to find somewhere else to live. We managed to rent a nice little weatherboard house near the Ocean Beach Hotel.

Mum and I began to disagree a lot more. I had bought myself a few things from my wages and she would give them away to her friends without even asking me. If they said they liked something, she'd say, 'Oh, Glad doesn't want that, she can buy another one, you take it.' People would come and deliberately point out something of mine and she would give it to them straight away, especially if they were white people. She was trying to buy white friends. It used to really upset me. There were so many things I didn't understand then.

I met Bill at the engagement party of one of my friends. All my teenage years, I'd dreamt of this man I would one day meet and marry, so it was quite a shock to see him at this party. The dreams I'd had about him were always mixed up. Sometimes, they'd turn into nightmares. My future marriage was to turn out like that, good and bad, only I didn't know it then. As soon as I was introduced to Bill, I knew my carefree days were over. I wasn't ready to settle down and get married, but I knew I didn't have any choice: this was meant to be.

Bill was different from the other men I'd gone out with; he was older, more worldly. I knew he'd been a prisoner-of-war in Germany, but I didn't realise then what a terrible time he'd had.

None of my friends liked Bill and Mum disapproved of him, too. 'He drinks too much,' she told me, 'you don't want to marry a drinker.' My friends tried to warn me about him. They said he was wild, sometimes crazy, but I didn't listen.

The day after I met Bill, he said, 'You're going to marry me.'

'No, I'm not,' I said.

'Yes, you are.'

I was going with someone else at the time, so I thought, well, I might be able to hold him off for a while, but it wasn't to be. We went out for a year before we married. Mum never changed her mind about him. I told him I was Aboriginal, but he said he didn't care. I don't think he did, then; later he changed. His parents disapproved of me. They didn't want him marrying a coloured person.

Mum didn't want to come to the wedding and neither did Bill's family, so we got married in a registry office. I was twenty-one. I think Mum had hoped it would all blow over and I'd get interested in someone else. She had always been very jealous of anyone who took my attention away from her. She wanted me to stay at home for the rest of my life and look after her.

Bill's War

After we were married, we lived with Mum. I was very happy. I continued to work at the florist shop.

Things didn't improve with Bill's family. They were very disappointed that he had married me. Bill's mother was narrow-minded, she used to say things to Bill behind my back. I knew she would never accept me as an equal. I don't know how much Bill's father worried about me being coloured.

Grandpa Milroy used to travel around putting in petrol bowsers for the Shell Oil Company and Bill's mother was always sending Bill off to the goldfields to haul his father out of the pubs and bring him home. Bill's father gambled away a fortune: he had Bill drinking beer from his early teenage years.

When Bill was fourteen, he'd run away from home and got a job up North as a stockman. He told everyone he was sixteen — he could pass for that because he was tall. He loved the life up there and was very upset when his father found him and made him return to Perth.

I found it difficult mixing with Bill's brothers and their friends. I'd been brought up strictly, whereas they lived in a brave new world. It was becoming a permissive society, even then.

Bill was different to his brothers. He had strong ideas and a kind heart. He had religious beliefs. He never talked about them, but I knew they were there, deep inside him. Sometimes, when he talked about the war, I felt that there was a spiritual force that helped him get through.

When I found out I was pregnant, I was really excited. Bill was overjoyed, expecting a son, but it was Sally. I couldn't believe that I finally had a family of my own. Mum was really pleased, too. In a strange way, I think it made her feel more secure to be a grandmother.

Not long after that Bill applied for a tradesman's flat down at Beaconsfield, where he was working as a plumber. We were pleased to be moving into our own place. The surroundings were very pretty; it had originally been a farm — everyone still called it Mulberry Farm. There was a huge mulberry tree opposite our flat and olive trees dotted all over the place.

When we first moved in, we were always broke, it made a difference, having to pay rent. I'd had to give up work when I became pregnant. Sally was very sick when she was small; we nearly lost her a couple of times.

Then Bill began having nightmares again. He'd suffered from them ever since he'd come back from the war. He'd scream and scream at night. Before we married, I had thought that the idea of being a POW was heroic and romantic; now I thought differently. I used to try to get him to talk about his nightmares, it helped him a little, but he'd never go really deeply into what had happened to him. It all got so bad that, in the end, I couldn't stand it. I took Sally and moved back in with Mum.

I'd been at her place about ten days when I started to worry about Bill. I still loved him. I've never told anyone Bill's war experiences, but perhaps it will help you to understand your father, Sally, if I write it down...

Bill fought in the desert with the 2/16th Battalion.

He said he found it so hard to kill other people. I remember him telling me about one time when there were Germans in the sandhills, outlined like sitting ducks in a shooting gallery. Bill was on the machine gun and the others called to him, 'Shoot them while you've got the chance!' He said he couldn't, it was too easy. Someone shoved him aside, grabbed the gun and mowed them down. It made him feel sick.

He was wounded and placed in the army hospital. That was how he got left behind in the Middle East, because the rest of his battalion was shipped back to fight in New Guinea. After he recovered, he was placed in the 2/28th and continued to fight in the desert.

Bill was captured at El Alamein. Along with two thousand other Allied prisoners, he was crammed into the holds of the *Nino Bixio*, an Italian freighter. Second day out to sea, they were torpedoed by an Allied submarine. Bill said he'd been sitting having a joke with the bloke next to him when a torpedo whizzed straight through, hit the other side of the hold, exploded and flung everyone back onto him. When he came to he was covered in blood. He thought he'd had it. The ship started taking water, and the steel ladders leading to the top part of the hold had been destroyed, so there was no way out.

Survivors from the top part of the hold threw down ropes and the Captain, a big, red-headed Italian, shouted, 'If anyone's alive down there, climb up!'

By the time Bill got himself out from underneath all the bodies, he realised he was actually still in one piece. He had bits of shrapnel embedded in his arms, legs and chest, but apart from that, he was all right. He picked up the nearest bloke to him and climbed the rope.

The next day, an Italian destroyer took them in tow. They beached on the Greek coast and the wounded were taken to shore and laid out along the beach. Bill said there'd been over five hundred men in their hold when they were hit. Only seventy survived the torpedo and a lot of them died on the beach.

Those that could walk were marched through the nearest town where men spat on them and women threw slops over them. They stayed in Corinth for a while, then they were shipped back to Italy and sent to a prisoner-of-war camp — Campo 57. Bill said the commandant there was a real Fascist, he wasn't like most Italians. He liked to see them suffer.

The Allies began bombing the area near the camp — that's when Bill escaped. The guards were so frightened they ran off, leaving the gates wide open. All the prisoners followed. Bill said to Abercrombe, the bloke that was with him, 'Not down the middle of the road, the Germans will realise we're being bombed and come to round us up. Get down in the ditch.'

Sure enough, a few minutes later, along came the Germans and herded everyone back inside. Bill and Abercrombe hid in the ditch till nightfall.

Abercrombe wanted to head south in the hope of meeting up with the Yanks, but Bill talked him into going north, to Switzerland. They travelled mainly at night, stealing food and sleeping in the fields.

Eventually they came to a small town and hung around the well in the centre of the village, hoping someone friendly would notice them. They knew the Germans were around, but so far they hadn't seen any, so they hoped their luck would hold out.

An old bloke came along and looked them over, Bill had picked up a few Italian words, so he told him who they were. The old man fetched the head man, who took them home to his place and gave them some warm food and *vino*. Bill asked him to put them in touch with the Resistance. He said they'd have to let him make a phone call. Bill listened carefully and realised he was really phoning the Germans. They nicked off before the Germans got there.

They kept travelling north, afraid to enter any town after

that. They were worn out, desperate. They entered another small town and, once again, hung around the well. When a woman came for water, Bill asked her if she could take them to the head man. It turned out it was her husband.

This time they were lucky; these Italians hated the war and the Germans. They took Bill and Abercrombe to a safe farm run by Guiseppe and Maria Bosso and their fourteen-year-old daughter, Edmea. Bill said they were wonderful people, full of guts. They treated him like a son. He learnt to speak Italian fluently and, because he looked like a northern Italian, he sometimes passed himself off as one, drinking *vino* and singing songs with the Germans in the tavern.

During the day, Bill worked in the fields with the other labourers. When they heard that the farms nearby were being searched for escaped POWs, Bill and Abercrombe would hide out down near a small creek. During this time, they lived on frogs, green snakes and berries. Eventually, they'd get word that the coast was clear and the whole village would have a big dance in one of the barns to celebrate the fact that they'd outwitted the Germans again. They'd all laugh and dance and drink too much *vino*.

One morning, the Bosso family were very upset, because they'd had word that the SS had burnt and slaughtered a whole village for sheltering POWs. The town had a meeting to decide what they were going to do. They all decided to continue hiding Allied prisoners, even if it meant losing the whole village. Bill said he told Guiseppe it was a risk he wouldn't let them take.

Guiseppe got in touch with the Underground, who said it would be better if they headed for Switzerland. They sent two members of the Resistance to guide Bill and Abercrombe over the Swiss Alps. Bill had his twenty-first birthday in the mountains. When they reached the border, the Swiss guards gave them hot chocolate and warm food. They told them if they crossed into Switzerland, they'd be there for the duration of the war, which could be years, but if they went back and joined up with the Yanks, it might only be a few months, because the Americans were making rapid progress advancing through Italy at that stage.

Bill didn't fancy sitting in Switzerland, he had too much spirit for that, so he asked the guides to take him and Abercrombe back to Italy. So they took them back over the mountains and then pointed them in the direction where the Yanks were supposed to be advancing.

That night, they came to a road and were about to cross, when Bill said, 'Don't, there's something wrong.' There was nothing in sight, but Bill had a premonition it was dangerous. He hid in the ditch and told Abercrombe to do the same.

Abercrombe was fed up by this stage, so he said, 'There's nothing there, I'm going.' He ran onto the road, but halfway across, a searchlight spotted him and he was gunned down. Bill said he was so shocked he just froze.

Finally, he forced himself to get going. He walked all night until he came to a river. He sat down amongst the reeds. He lay down and was half-asleep when he heard the sound of barking dogs coming closer and closer. Germans, he thought. He started to run. A bullet whizzed past his head, missing him by only a few inches. He stopped and turned with his hands in the air.

To his relief, it was only the Italian police. He spoke swiftly and told them he was a labourer on his way to work at a nearby farm. They said, 'You're no labourer, you're a murderer. You're wanted in Rome for killing many women.' They showed him a poster with a picture of the wanted man. Bill said he couldn't believe it; the man was his double. He was forced, then, to tell them who he really was.

'You shouldn't have run,' they said, 'we would have let you go. We can't now, because we have to account to the Germans for every bullet we use. If we let you go, they'll know. We have to think of our families, we're sorry.'

Bill was handed over to the SS. They questioned and tortured him for days on end, asking where he had been, and who had helped him. Bill said he would rather have died than tell them. He was like that. He was a very proud man and very stubborn.

Every day, he heard the firing squad in operation; every

day, he wondered if he would be next. They always walked past his cell with their victims. If they turned left past his cell, he knew it was an execution. If they turned right they were transferring the prisoner somewhere else.

One morning, they came for him. He thought, *this is it, I'm going to die*. He thought they must have decided to give up questioning him and shoot him instead.

At the end of the corridor, Bill turned left and the guard butted him in the back with his rifle, knocking him to the floor. Bill rose and felt the guard's rifle hard in his back. 'Turn right! You are being transferred to Germany.'

He was taken to the office, where he was handed over to another guard.

On the way to the train, the guard said, 'Don't try to escape and we'll get along fine.' Bill was surprised he spoke in English. He boarded the train in the company of this guard and two SS officers.

The German guard gave him a cigarette and said quietly, 'Speak in English, the SS can't understand.' He confided to Bill that he had been educated in England. He said he hated the SS, he called them animals. He warned Bill to watch out for the youngest officer. 'Don't try to escape. He'll use any excuse to shoot you.'

This guard was the one who accompanied Bill to the POW camp. Before he handed him over, he gave Bill a heavy overcoat and some good boots. 'Never barter these,' he said, 'you won't survive without them.'

Bill was taken to Stalag 7A in Moosburg, then transferred to Stalag 8C in Sagan.

In the Sagan camp he had to work in the local coal mines — long hours and damp, dangerous work. He developed a bad chest infection, so they said he could do easier work and sent him to dig potatoes out of the frozen fields. Bill said it was easier down the mines. The only advantage working in the fields was if you could pinch a potato and use it in camp for bargaining. They were fed on vegetable soup which was just water. Once a month, the soup had meat in it, a horse's head.

Some of the guards at Sagan were really brutal. They loved to burst in at midnight, tell the men to strip, then stand them at attention in the snow. The worse the war went, the meaner they became. One day, they assembled the men and told them they were going to hand out Red Cross packages. They tipped out Nestles milk, jam, tea, cigarettes into a pile, then mashed the whole lot up together. 'Now,' they said, 'you can't complain you didn't get your Red Cross parcels!' After that, they told the prisoners they had to eat it; it was a big joke to the guards.

Then they informed the prisoners they were going to march to another camp. There had been rumours that the Russians were advancing. The end of the war in Europe was near. They were marched fifty miles to Spremberg, then forced to march another three hundred miles to Duderstadt. It was very cold and they had to sleep out in the snow. There was no food; they had to find what they could by the side of the road. Bill said even the German people were starving by then. When they stopped near one village, an old German peasant woman ran up to him and shoved a stale piece of black bread into his hand. A guard shot her in the back. Bill said that guard was a real bastard and would use any excuse to use his rifle.

A lot of prisoners died of cold and were just left by the side of the road. Bill was really glad he hadn't traded his heavy overcoat.

When they reached Duderstadt, the conditions were terrible. The camp was infested with lice and there was only one latrine for over a thousand men. Prisoners were dying like flies from dysentery and pneumonia. After another few days, there was a rumour that the Yanks were close.

Then, early one morning, a tank broke down the gates of the camp and a sandy-headed Yank popped up and said, 'Any of you guys want some ginger cake and ice-cream?'

Bill said the men that had any energy left just cried and cried. The Yank in charge couldn't believe the state they were all in. They were all airlifted to France, where they were given medical treatment before being transferred to England. Bill spent six months in hospital in England before he was fit to sail home.

I thought about everything Bill told me after I returned to live with my mother. I knew that was just the tip of the iceberg, he hadn't told me the whole story.

By the time I'd been with Mum three weeks, he came around to beg me to come back to him. I knew then that if I did, it was for ever, I couldn't leave him again. I had to go back. He had no one. I still loved him. I thought maybe I could help make up for what he'd been through.

It turned out I was wrong. I couldn't heal his mind, it was too damaged. They hadn't broken his spirit or his will to live, but they'd broken his mind. He had a sensitive side to him and they'd destroyed that. He couldn't get away from what was inside him. He couldn't escape from his own memories.

A Road Like Mine

In no time at all, Jilly was born, my second child.

Bill was trying hard to hold himself together, but there were still times when he'd go off on a drinking binge and I wouldn't see him for a few days. On these occasions, Mum would come and stay just to keep me company.

She was doing housework now. I was glad, because it was easier for her. She was always buying clothes for the kids and dropping in groceries. She knew I had no money.

Bill had a nervous breakdown and they put him in Hollywood Hospital. He couldn't cope with any pressure or responsibility. I used to feel awful when I visited him. Eventually he was sent home with drugs that were supposed to keep him calm.

By the time Jill was four months old, I was pregnant again. Then a polio epidemic hit Mulberry Farm. I caught it. Mum moved in with us. Bill was working at the time and I needed someone to look after Sally and Jilly. By some miracle, I recovered from the polio.

I gave birth to Billy that November. Of course, Bill was overjoyed that he had a son at last.

Bill applied for a State Housing home in Manning. Mum was living with us permanently now. I really needed her help with three little ones so close together and Bill the way he was. When Billy was six months old, we moved to Manning.

There was a large swamp at the back of us, alive with wildlife, turtles, frogs, gilgies, grey cranes. It reminded me of the bush from my own childhood days. I encouraged the children to take an interest in the wildlife. It was good for them to learn about nature and how important it is to our lives.

We'd only been in Manning a month when Mum began to complain about all the Aborigines living in the swamp. 'Did you hear that music last night?' she said. 'They been having corroborees every night, I think I'll go down there and tell them all off.'

I often sat and listened to it with her after that. I've never been to a corroboree, but that music had always been inside me. When I was little, I was told Aboriginal music was heathen music. I thought it was beautiful music; whenever I heard it, it was like a message, as though I was being supported, protected.

One night, I told Mum there were no Aborigines in the swamp. She'd been complaining she couldn't sleep and she was sick of those blackfellas having a party every night. I don't think she believed me. 'You heard the music, Glad,' she said.

'There's no one down there,' I told her, 'it's a spiritual thing.' After that, we just accepted it. She'd sit out and listen to it and then go to bed. We didn't hear it every night, but it was there on and off right up until Bill died. Then it stopped.

Mum heard this other thing, too, she said there was a crocodile in the swamp. We only heard that noise at night. She'd tell the kids to be careful when they went down the swamp, to watch out for the crocodile. Sally and Jilly were always nicking off. I remember Mum saying to Sally, 'Aren't you scared of meeting that crocodile?' I couldn't help laughing, because I knew that was why Sally kept going down there, she *wanted* to meet him.

Bill seemed to pull himself together when we first went to the Manning house. I began to hope for a better future for us all. He managed to get a good job and cut down on his drinking. On the weekends, he worked for the Italian market gardeners in Spearwood. He loved mixing with them and speaking Italian. He had never forgotten the kindness of the Bossos during the war. He'd come home loaded up with fruit and vegetables and bottles of *vino*. He often did jobs for them free of charge. I think he felt indebted to all Italian people because they'd been so good to him.

Pretty soon, there were other houses going up around us. A widow with three children moved in at the back of us. Grace was such a nice person and Mum often had a chat and a cup of tea with her.

One morning, Bill was sitting on the bus going to work, when the chap next to him said, 'You look a sight better than the last time I saw you!'

Bill said, 'Do I know you?'

'You only saved my life, you bastard,' the man replied. It was Frank Potter, the man Bill had dragged up from the hold of the torpedoed ship. It turned out he and his wife lived only a few streets away. They saw a lot of each other after that.

Bill began having nightmares again. It seemed that things would just start going right for us, then the whole circle would start all over again. We were desperate, we'd gone through Mum's savings and Bill had hocked everything we had of value and spent the money on drink.

There were times when it was like something had taken him over. I really got frightened then, because I didn't know what was going to happen. He'd yell and scream and tell us all to get out of the house or he'd kill us. It was as though he'd suddenly turned into a stranger. Mum and I would run with the children to Grace's house. She was good to us, she knew we had nowhere else to go. Once he went to sleep, he was all right, we'd go back home then. When we returned in the morning, Bill would have no idea of what had happened. When I told him, he'd get really scared and commit himself to Hollywood again.

One winter, just after Bill had come out of hospital, it was really cold. Sally had been sick with croup, the river had flooded and water covered over half of our backyard. The house was damp right through, even though we had fires going day and night. Several of the houses near us were evacuated and the people given alternative accommodation.

We had no money for blankets, so we usually all ended up in the double bed. It meant we were warm, but no one got any sleep. 'We've got to get blankets for the children,' I told Bill.

'Doesn't the Canteen's Trust Fund give money to ex-servicemen in dire circumstances?'

Bill was very proud, he hated asking for help. Finally, he wrote to them. We waited eagerly for their reply. When it came, they said we weren't desperate enough. I was really disgusted, it was the same old story. It had taken years before the Repatriation Department would even give Bill a partial pension, because they considered him a malingerer.

No one understood in those days, if you'd lost an arm and a leg, you had no worries, but if there was something wrong with your mind, you were a malingerer. It made me feel sorry for the Vietnam veterans, fighting the same attitudes.

When Billy was just over two years old, I became pregnant again. It was a really bad time to have another child. I lay in bed at night, unable to sleep. I'd prayed and prayed and I'd got no answers. My usual capacity for overcoming my problems seemed to have deserted me. I knew I would have to give up my part-time job and I wondered how on earth we'd put food on the table. Bill had been in hospital on and off for months. He seemed happy with his weekend passes to come home; that way, he had no worry. He was drifting deeper and deeper into the protection of the hospital.

Bill came out of hospital about two months before the baby was due. This time, he really tried to help himself. I hoped that he would stay on his feet a bit longer this time, and he did. He started to work again and was looking forward to the baby.

I had a very difficult time giving birth to David. I nearly died. But David was a beautiful baby. Bill came to visit me in hospital, and was very distressed that I'd had a bad time. He always blamed himself when things went wrong.

When David was very small, Mum's brother Arthur, with his wife, Adeline, and their children, popped in to visit us. It was the first time I had seen Arthur in years and years. Mum and I were terribly excited.

Bill was lying down at the time. 'Come and meet Arthur and his family,' I said, 'you'll like them.'

'I don't want to meet them,' he said. 'I don't want to know them.'

I was really hurt, I knew if they had been white, he would have come out straight away. Bill was a strange man, he wasn't prejudiced against other racial groups, just Aboriginals. It wasn't like that when I first knew him.

Now he never liked us having our people to the house. We had to cut ourselves off. I think it was his upbringing. A friend called Jean White used to come and stay with us sometimes. He never minded her, because she was very light. Jean could pass for anything.

Bill went back into hospital and I began my regular visits to him again. I always took Sally, and sometimes I'd take Billy and Jill as well.

I suppose many people must wonder why on earth I didn't just take the kids and leave. Well, I nearly did, on several occasions, but Bill always threatened me. He said if I left him, he'd make sure the children were taken off me. He said, 'Nobody will let someone like you bring up kids and you know it. I'm the one that'll get custody, I'll give them to my parents.'

I knew what he meant. I always had a sinking feeling in my stomach when he said that. Aboriginal women weren't allowed to keep children fathered by a white man. He was right, I couldn't take the chance of losing them, I had to stay and try to cope somehow. They were all I had.

In April 1959, my daughter Helen was born.

Even though Bill was sick at the time, he managed to drive me to hospital. He looked so ill, it made me sad. I told him not to visit me, just to ring, I knew it'd be too much for him otherwise. He started crying, he felt useless, as though he was no good to any of us. That bloody war, I thought. I kissed his cheek and patted his hand. I tried to convey the message that I understood, that I didn't blame him. I knew Helen would be my last child. I knew I wouldn't have Bill much longer.

One night in October, ten months later, Bill came into the lounge-room where I was sitting by myself. I found I needed small moments alone to renew my strength and I only usually got these times after the children were well and truly asleep.

'I feel odd, Glad,' he said. 'I can't get warm. I feel as though I'm not really here, it's like I'm fading away.' I jumped up and felt him. He was cold. I felt his spirit had left his body. I knew then he was going to die.

Bill sat down and we talked into the early hours of the morning. It was strange, it was suddenly as though he was his old self, as though he'd been released from something. We talked about the children and we laughed. Bill said he hadn't felt so good in a long time. He said he knew tomorrow would be a new beginning for all of us.

Bill was in such a good mood at breakfast that he kept Billy home from school, so he and David and Billy could all have a game of footy together.

I left for work.

A neighbour rang me at twelve that day to tell me Bill had died. I was shocked. I went home immediately, but couldn't pull myself together. I walked around in a daze. If it hadn't been for Mrs Mainwaring, a neighbour, I don't know what I would have done. She told the children about their father. I don't know if they understood or not. It's hard enough for an adult to understand death.

A fortnight after Bill's death, I went back to work. I had a lot of bills to pay.

We were given a Legatee who was a real godsend. He was able to get my insurance policy paid out and that covered a lot of our debts. I applied for a war pension and was granted it. Actually, if I hadn't been so desperate, I would have refused it. I felt the whole department had been so mean to Bill. They'd done nothing for him while he was alive. Why did someone have to die before they recognised the seriousness of the problem?

Although I still grieved for Bill, I felt as though a load had been lifted from my shoulders. I was much more relaxed, I didn't have to worry about money and the children could make as much noise as they liked. Poor little kids, they needed all the love they could get.

Sally told me she'd overheard two of the teachers talking at school and it had made her angry. 'Who do they think they are?' she asked me. 'We don't want their pity. Don't they understand it's better he's gone?' She'd been close to her father, but she also knew what he was like. In some ways, they were similar; they were both rebels.

Bill had only been dead a short time when a Welfare lady came out to visit us. I was really frightened because I thought, if she realised we were Aboriginal, she might have the children taken away. We only had two bedrooms and a sleepout and there were five children, as well as Mum and me.

This woman asked me all sorts of questions and walked through our house with her nose in the air like a real snob. She asked where we all slept, and when I told her Helen slept with me, she was absolutely furious. She said, 'You are to get that child out of your bed, we will not stand for that. You work something else out, the children aren't to be in the same room as you. I'll come back and check to make sure you've got another bed.'

I just agreed with everything she said. I didn't want her to have any excuse to take the children off me.

It was after the visit from the Welfare lady that Mum and I decided we would definitely never tell the children they were Aboriginal. We were both convinced they would have a bad time, otherwise. Also, if word got out, another Welfare person might come and take them away. Mum said she didn't want the children growing up with people looking down on them. I understood what she meant. Aboriginals were treated the lowest of the low. It was as though they were the one race on earth that had nothing to offer.

When I was little, Mum had always pinched my nose and said, 'Pull your nose, Gladdie, pull it hard. You don't want to end up with a big nose like mine.' She was always pulling the kids' noses too. She wanted them to grow up to look like white people.

I suppose, looking back now, it seems awful that we deprived them of that heritage, but we thought we were doing the right thing at the time. With Bill gone, we now had some hope of a future and I knew he would want the children to get on in the world.

I took on any job that was going, I wasn't afraid to work. Sometimes I had four jobs on the go. I forced myself to learn how to drive, even though I was petrified of the thought of actually going on the road. I knew I would need that independence and it meant I could take the children on outings. They hadn't had much up until then.

After I'd managed to pay off all the extra debts, our lives really began to change. Now I never had to worry about where the next meal was coming from, and I could buy the kids lollies and fruit. Sometimes, we even went to the pictures.

I also found that, now we were on our own, I worried less about Mum. She would always have a home with me, and there was enough money for all of us to get by on. Best of all, she had her own family now. All her life, she'd had to mother

other people's children. Now she had her own flesh and blood. I hoped that would make up for some of her past.

When the opportunity to buy my own florist business came up, I grabbed it. I had always wanted to be my own boss. My old friend Lois gave me a loan. She knew I would pay her back. I soon had that shop on its feet and doing twice as well as when the previous owners had it. It gave me a new independence and something to be proud of. Also, it gave us the extra money we needed to get us through the children's teenage years.

I'm very proud of my children and the way they turned out.

I feel embarrassed now, to think that once I wanted to be white. As a child, I even hoped a white family would adopt me, a rich one, of course. I've changed since those days.

I'm still a coward, though. When a stranger asks me what nationality I am, I sometimes say a Heinz variety. I feel bad when I do that. It's because there are still times when I'm scared inside, scared to say who I really am.

But at least I've made a start. And I hope my children will feel proud of the spiritual background from which they've sprung. If we all keep saying we're proud to be Aboriginal, then maybe other Australians will see that we are a people to be proud of. I suppose every mother wants her children to achieve something. All I want my children to do is to pass their Aboriginal heritage on.

I suppose, in hundreds of years' time, there won't be any black Aboriginals left. Our colour dies out; as we mix with other races, we'll lose some of the physical characteristics that distinguish us now. I like to think that, no matter what we become, our spiritual tie with the land and the other unique qualities we possess will somehow weave their way through to future generations of Australians. This is our land, after all; surely we've got something to offer.

It hasn't been an easy task, baring my soul. I'd rather have kept hidden things which have now seen the light of day. But, like everything else in my life, I knew I had to do it. I find

I'm embarrassed sometimes by what I have told, but I know I cannot retract what has been written, it's no longer mine.

The only way I can explain it is by one of my favourite rules, which I haven't always followed. Let me pass this way but once and do what good I can. I shall not pass this way again. Maybe someone else is walking a road that's like mine.

3

SOMETHING SERIOUS

It took several months to work through Mum's story. During that time, many tears were shed. We became very close. When she talked about Dad's war experiences, I remembered how, when I was a child, Dad used to tell me about some of the things that had happened to him. I always wanted to hear the story about the horse's head soup. And I remember the day Frank Potter, the soldier Dad rescued when the Italian ship was torpedoed, turned up at our house, and how he and Dad sat yarning and drinking together. And, of course, I remembered very well visiting Dad in hospital, and also those scary times when he seemed to become a frightening stranger, and the rest of us would decamp to our neighbour's house until he calmed down.

Although Mum had finally shared her story with me, she still couldn't bring herself to tell my brothers and sisters. Consequently, I found myself communicating it to them in bits and pieces as seemed appropriate. It was, and still is, upsetting for us all. We all found it difficult to come to terms with the experiences Mum had been through.

By the beginning of June 1983, Nan's health wasn't too good.

'You've got to take her to the doctor,' I told Mum one day.
'You know how she hates doctors.'
'But what if it's something serious?'

Mum took Nan to see our local doctor a few days later. They sent Nan for a chest X-ray, which revealed that one of her lungs had collapsed.

When Mum phoned through the news to me, I said gently, 'I think you should prepare yourself, Mum. I'm not trying to make a big deal out of this, but I think it will be serious.'

'You mean you think she might die?'

'Yes.'

'You don't know what you're talking about, Sally! It's only a collapsed lung, they can fix that! She has to go into hospital in two days' time for tests.'

The night before Nan was due to go into hospital, she stayed at my place.

I made Nan a cup of tea and we sat in the lounge-room to talk. 'I'd like you to listen to a story, Nan,' I said, 'it's only a couple of pages.'

'Oooh, I like a good story.'

Before I recorded my mother's story on cassette, I had persuaded Nan's brother, Arthur, to talk about his memories of his early life at Corunna Downs Station, where he and Nan were born, as well as his later experiences. Arthur was very old when he told me his story; he died soon after it was finished. Now I read Nan the part of this story where he described how he used to take part in boxing shows at fairgrounds. I didn't tell Nan the story was Arthur's — not at first, anyway. When I stopped, she said, 'That's a wonderful story, a really good one.'

'This is what I've been writing, Nan. That's Arthur's story.'

'I can't believe it! That's Arthur's story? I didn't know he had a good story like that. You got to keep that story safe. Read me some more.'

I read a little more, and then we began to talk about the old days and life on Corunna Downs Station. For some reason, Nan was keen to talk. As she went on, her breath began to come in shorter and shorter gasps. Her words tumbled out one over the other, as if her tongue couldn't say them quickly enough.

I could see that she was very tired. 'Would you like to lie down for a while now?' I asked.

She sighed. 'Yes, I think I will.'

I took Nan into her bedroom and she climbed into bed. After I'd settled the children down, I walked quietly past the bedroom door. I expected her to be asleep, but she wasn't.

'Sally,' she called. 'Come here.'

'What is it?'

'I want to tell you more about the station.' I nearly stopped her, she could hardly breathe, but how could I tell her not to talk when it had taken a lifetime for her to get to this point?

I listened quietly as she spoke about wild ducks and birds, the blue hills and all the fruit that grew along the creek. Her eyes had a faraway look and her face was very soft. I kept smiling at her because she was smiling at me, but inside, I wanted to cry. I'd seen that look before, on Arthur's face. I knew she was going to die. Nan finally settled down and closed her eyes.

When I visited Nan in hospital the following evening, she was very bright. Mum had been there on and off all day.

'Hi, Nan,' I said as I walked up to her bed. 'How are they treating you?'

'The nurses are lovely.'

'How's the tucker?'

'Very good. They gave me meat and casserole and a soup and a lovely caramel sweet.'

'Well, I'm glad they're treating you right, Nan. I brought some more of Arthur's story to read. Do you want to listen, or are you too tired?'

'Read it!' She folded her hands in her lap and leaned back against the pillows, waiting for me to begin. It was a long chapter, so I only read her half. As I read, Nan 'oohed' and 'aahed' in the appropriate places.

'I'll read you the rest tomorrow night,' I said.

'That's a good idea.'

'You look tired, do you want to sleep now?'

'I'd better. They're putting that thing down my throat tomorrow.'

'I know, that's why you need a good sleep.'

We had to wait a day for the results of the bronchoscopy. I decided to spend the day at Jill's because it was near the hospital, and I wanted to be on the spot when we got the news.

We were fortunate. One of Mum's dreams had been fulfilled: our sister Helen had studied medicine and was doing her residency at the hospital, so she was able to get the results for us straight away. We had a doctor in the family at last.

Mum and I were sitting at the kitchen table having some lunch when Jill came back from answering the front door.

'I think you should prepare yourself,' she said to Mum. 'Helen's just come home in tears, she's in her room.'

Mum and I rushed into Helen's room. Jill took all the children into the lounge-room for a game of snakes-and-ladders.

Helen sat on the edge of her bed, crying. When she saw us, she murmured, 'She's got a tumour. I suspected it all along, but I guess I was hoping it was something else.'

Mum began to cry. I couldn't find any tissues, so I passed her a towel.

'How long?' I asked.

'They haven't completed the tests yet. We won't know until tomorrow afternoon.'

I told the news to Jill, then made a cup of tea for Mum and Helen.

Mum gulped hers down, then went into Jill's room to cry on her own.

I left her for half an hour, then went in to find her still sprawled across the bed, crying her heart out.

'She's expecting me this afternoon,' Mum sobbed when she saw me. 'I told her I'd go down.'

'Would you like me to go?'

'Are you sure you'll be all right?'

'I'll be all right.'

'You go then. I'll probably be okay by tonight, I'll see her then.'

Helen came with me to the hospital. As we mounted the stairs that led to Nan's ward, Helen began to cry again.

'You going to be okay?' I asked.

'I'll be all right,' she murmured.

When we reached Nan's bed, she was lying on her back in a hospital gown. She was very hot; under the oxygen mask, her breathing was laboured.

The doctor was there. We both sat down beside the bed. Helen held Nan's hand. She seemed to be slipping in and out of consciousness. It was too much for Helen; tears began to flow silently down her cheeks. She reached for a tissue, and just as she was wiping her face, Nan opened her eyes and said, 'What's wrong, Helen?'

'Nothing,' she replied, and looked away. Nan looked straight at me. I looked back. I was only confirming what she already knew inside herself.

We stayed for a few hours and left when Nan was asleep.

The rest of the results came through the following afternoon and Mum was called to the hospital to discuss them. I visited again that night. To my surprise, I found Nan sitting up in bed, eating tea. She looked much better.

After that, we laughed and talked and joked for over an hour about old times. We talked about all sorts of little things — how we used to say that if the lawnmower man didn't come soon, the grass would be so high we wouldn't be able to see the house.

Finally, Mum said, 'Well, we'd better go now. It's getting late.'

'Are you going too, Sally?' Nan asked. She gave me one of her looks. I knew she wanted to talk to me alone.

'I have to go now, Nan,' I told her, 'but I promise you that we are going to have a good talk over the weekend.'

The doctors advised radiotherapy for Nan. They said it could prolong her life for another six months, though they couldn't guarantee this. Mum wanted her to have the therapy, and so did Helen. Nan herself said she didn't want it. I agreed with her — I knew she didn't realise the side-effects that could occur. And I felt that Nan was more afraid of hospitals than of dying.

Finally, after a very bad experience in the hospital, when Nan was used without her consent as a subject for a practice exam for hospital registrars, we definitely decided against the radiotherapy. She left hospital a few days later and came home.

'It was terrible, Sally, that experience,' Nan told me. 'I'm never goin' back there. And I'm not havin' that treatment.'

4

GOOD NEWS

The following Monday, Mum arrived early at my place with Nan. We had decided that it was best if Nan stayed with me each day during the week while Mum was at work.

Nan brought her black bag laden with biscuits and lollies for the kids.

'I've got a surprise for you, Nan,' I said. 'Paul and I cleaned out the sleepout. We've put a bed in there for you and a table. That way, you can have an afternoon sleep without the kids disturbing you. Come and look.'

'Ooh, doesn't it look nice!' She smiled as she peered through the doorway.

'You've got the louvres, so you'll get plenty of fresh air if you want.'

When Mum came to pick Nan up that afternoon, she said, 'Well, had a good day?'

'A lovely quiet day, Gladdie.'

'You ready to go home, then?'

Nan looked from me to Mum. 'I think I'll stay a few more days.'

Mum was aghast. 'You can't be here all the time, Sally's got a baby to look after. She can't have you as well.'

'I don't mind, Mum. She can stay.'

'It's settled, then,' said Nan.

I took Mum out to show her the sleepout.

'Are you sure this isn't going to be too much for you?' she asked me.

'Even if it is, won't be for long.'

'The doctors couldn't say exactly how long, could be six months, nine months.'

'No, Mum, I think she'll go well before Christmas.'

'I don't like it when you talk like that. It's as though you want her to die.'

'I suppose I do, in a way, but only because I think it's what she wants.'

'You haven't talked like this to Nan, have you?'

'No.'

We walked back into the lounge-room.

'What do you think?' asked Nan.

'Very nice,' replied Mum. 'When do you want me to pick you up?'

'Oh, make it Wednesday — that all right, Sally?'

'Whenever you like.'

When Mum came back on Wednesday, Nan told her she wasn't going home.

'This isn't your home,' Mum argued, 'this is Sally's house. The dogs are missing you, and the cats.'

'Look, Gladdie,' Nan said, 'I wheel the baby when he's crying and I've done a bit of raking in the garden. Sally can't do it all. I'll stay here till Friday and then I'll come home for the weekend.'

I walked Mum to her car. 'Don't worry about her, Mum,' I said, 'she's having a good time.'

Nan kept her word and went home for the weekend. On Sunday, Mum rang.

'Hi, Mum, what's up? Nan's not worse, is she?'

'No, she's as bright as a button. She wants to know if she can live with you during the week and come home to me on weekends.'

'Yeah, that's fine,' I replied.

I heard a voice in the background and then Mum saying, 'Yes, it's all right, you can live with Sally.'

'You know, Mum,' I said, 'I think she likes being here so she can complain about you.'

Over the next few weeks, our lives fell into a pattern that tended to revolve around Nan and the baby. Amber and Blaze loved having Nan live with us. Not only did they have an unlimited supply of goodies, they also had a captive audience before whom they could perform all the television advertisements they had learnt by heart.

Every night, Amber read Nan a bedtime story. The stories were about Aboriginal children in the Western Desert. Nan loved to listen to them, and when Amber was finished reading, she'd tell about some of the things she'd done as a child.

Blaze was particularly horrified one night when she told him how tasty witchetty grubs were. 'Hmmn,' she said, 'you gobble them up. They good tucker, real good tucker.'

Blaze returned to me in the kitchen with a rather green look on his face. 'Did ya hear what she said?' he asked.

'I heard.'

'Have you ever eaten them, Mum?'

'No. But when you were a baby, you used to eat snails.'

'Aw yuk! Don't tell me any more!'

'All right,' I laughed. A few minutes later, Blaze returned to the kitchen and whispered, 'Don't tell Nan about the snails. She might give me them instead of lollies.'

Nan and the children became very close. The three of them spent hours closeted away in her room. Even though Blaze was only five, he treated Nan like a real lady, worrying over where she was going to sit and whether she was warm enough. Whenever I wanted Blaze, I knew where to look; on the end of Nan's bed.

'Blaze,' I said to him one day, 'Nan's tired. She's supposed to be having her afternoon sleep and you're in here talking.'

'She's all right, Mum,' he answered confidently, 'aren't you, Nan? I'm telling her stories.'

One afternoon, after his usual session with Nan, he

strolled into the kitchen and garbled out a set of instructions in what, to me, sounded like a foreign language.

'What was that?'

'That's what Nan taught me,' he said, smiling. He was obviously very proud of himself. 'You know how we speak English? Well, that's what she speaks.'

'I see. And what does it mean?'

'It means get me a drink!'

I laughed and poured him a drink of cordial. He gulped it down quickly. 'Gotta go now, Mum. That was just a practice. She's gunna teach me more.'

Then, one afternoon, just after we'd finished lunch, Nan said, 'You still doin' that book?'

'Yep.'

'Arthur's story was real good.'

'Yours could be like that.'

'Oooh, no, I got secrets, Sally. I don't want anyone to know.'

'I don't like secrets. Not when they're the sort of secrets you could use to help your own people.'

'It wouldn't make no difference.'

'That's what everyone says. No one will talk. Don't you see, Nan, someone's got to tell. Otherwise, things will stay the same, they won't get any better.'

'Course they won't talk, Sally. They frightened. You don't know what it was like. You're too young.'

'I'm not too young to understand. If you'd just tell me a little.'

'That's just it, you dunno what you're doin' writin' this book. Bad things might happen to you. If I tell you some things, next thing, you'll be tellin' everyone, I know what you're like.'

'You don't have to worry about me. I can take care of myself.'

Nan paused and looked at me shrewdly. She was quiet for a minute or so, then she said, 'Maybe I will tell you some things.'

'Really?' I couldn't believe it.
'I don't want to tell you everything.'
'You don't have to.'
'I can keep my secrets?'
'Yeah.'
'All right. I tell you some things, but that's all.'
'You want to start now?'
'Aah,' she sighed, 'I'm tired now. Tomorrow.'

When Blaze came home from pre-school that afternoon, the first thing he said to Nan was, 'C'mon, Nan, let's go to your room.'

Nan laughed. 'You just after more lollies,' she said.

'No I'm not, Nan, honest. I want to tell you what I said for news at school.'

'Well, can't I hear your news, too?' I asked.

'Okay. I stood out the front and I said, "I've got some good news this morning. I'd like you all to know I got a bit of blackfella in me."'

Nan burst out laughing and so did I.

'Why are you laughing?'

'We're not, darling, we're not.' I smiled. 'That was good news. What did the kids say?'

'Ah, nothin', but later on, Stewart wanted to know which bit, and I didn't know what to say.'

That night, Mum made her usual phone call to check on how Nan was going.

'She's fine,' I said. 'And I've got good news.'

'What?'

'She's agreed to talk.'

'You're joking.'

'Nope. She's going to start tomorrow. Mind you, she says she's still going to keep her secrets, but anything's better than nothing.'

'You know, I think it was because we had an argument over the weekend.'

'What did you argue about?'

'Oh, the same old thing, the past. I told her she never realised what a lonely little girl I was. I asked her to tell me about my grandmother and she said, "You don't want to know about her, she was black!" '

'What did you say?'

'I said I didn't care what colour she was. I never knew anything about her till Arthur started talking. I've always wanted a family and she deprived me of even knowing I had a grandmother. I started to cry, you see, couldn't stop. That upset her. Maybe she's been thinking about that.'

'Could be. Did you ask about your sister again?'

'Yes, of course I did, but she always gets so upset when I ask about that.'

'She didn't tell you anything, then?'

'Not a thing. You will tell me what she says, won't you?'

'Of course.'

The following morning, I set up my recorder and, after a cup of tea, Nan and I sat down to talk.

'What do you want me to say?' Nan asked.

'Anything. Just tell me what you want to. Maybe you could start with Corunna Downs.'

'Righto.' I waited patiently as Nan sat staring at the recorder. 'You sure that thing's on? I can't hear it.'

'You only hear it when I play something back.'

'Oh. You sure you'll get my voice on it?' When I burst out laughing, she asked: 'What you laughin' at?'

'You! A few weeks ago, you were threatening to hide this recorder and now you're worried you won't get on it.'

Nan looked a little sheepish. 'Ah well, that's the way of it,' she chuckled.

5

DAISY CORUNNA'S STORY

(1900–1983)

Talahue

My name is Daisy Corunna, I'm Arthur's sister. My Aboriginal name is Talahue. I can't tell you when I was born, but I feel old. My mother had me on Corunna Downs Station, just out of Marble Bar. She said I was born under a big old gum tree and the midwife was called Diana. Course, that must have been her whitefella name. All the natives had whitefella and tribal names. When I was comin' into the world, a big mob of kids stood round waitin' for to get a look at me. I bet they got a fright.

I was happy up North. I had my mother and there was Old Fanny, my grandmother. Gladdie 'minds me of Old Fanny, she's got the same crooked smile. They both got round faces like the moon, too. I 'member Old Fanny always wore a handkerchief on her head with little knots tied all the way around. Sometimes, my granddaughter Helen 'minds me of her, too. They both short and giggly with skinny legs. Aah, she was good for a laugh, Old Fanny.

She loved panning for tin. All the old people panned for tin. You could see it lyin' in the dirt, heavy and dark, like black marbles. Old Fanny said I had good eyes, sometimes she took me with her for luck. We traded the tin for sugar or flour.

Old Fanny went pink-eye* to Hillside one day. I never saw her again. They tell me she died on Hillside, maybe she knew she was going to die. She was a good old grandmother.

On the station, I went under the name Daisy Brockman. It wasn't till I was older that I took the name Corunna. Now, some people say my father wasn't Howden Drake-Brockman, they say he was this man from Malta. What can I say? Aah, you see, that's the trouble with us blackfellas, we don't know who we belong to, no one'll own up. I got to be careful what I say. You can't put no lies in a book.

Course, I had another father, he wasn't my real father like, but he looked after us just the same. Chinaman was his name. He was very tall and strong. The people respected him. They were scared of him. He was Arthur's Aboriginal father, too. He was a powerful man.

My poor mother lost a lot of babies. I had two sisters that lived, Lily and Rosie. They were, what do they call it? Fullblood, yes. I was the light one of the family, the little one with blonde hair. Of course, there was Arthur, but they took him away when I was just a baby.

I 'member Old Pompee, he was the old boy that looked after the vegetable garden. He told me my mother cried and cried when they took Arthur. She kept callin' to him like. Callin' to him to come back. The people thought Arthur was gettin' educated so he could run the station some day. They thought it'd be good to have a blackfella runnin' the station. They was all wrong. My poor old mother never saw him again.

* *pink-eye* — term used by Aboriginal people of north-west Australia, similar to the more widely known term walkabout. A period of wandering as a nomad, often as undertaken by Aborigines who feel the need to leave the place where they are in contact with white society, and return for spiritual replenishment to their traditional way of life. Can also simply mean a holiday, usually without leave.

Rosie and I was close. Lily was older than me. I spent a lot of time with Rosie. I was very sad when she died. She was only young. My mother nursed her, did everything for her, but we lost her. Good old Rosie, you know I been thinkin' 'bout her lately.

I'll tell you a story about our white man's names. My mother was in Hedland with the three of us when an English nursing sister saw her near the well. She said, 'Have you got names for your three little girls?'

Mum said, 'No.'

She said, 'Well, I'll give you names, real beautiful ones. We'll call this one Lily, this one Rosie and this little one Daisy.' We didn't mind being called that, we thought we were pretty flowers.

I haven't told you about my brother Albert yet. He was light, too. He used to tease me. He'd chase me, then he'd hide behind a big bush and jump out and pretend he was the devil-devil. Oooh, he was naughty to me. They took Albert when they took Arthur, but Albert got sick and came back to the station. He was a good worker. He liked playing with me. He called me his little sister.

They was a good mob on Corunna. A real good mob. I been thinkin' 'bout all of them lately. There was Peter Linck, the well-sinker. I think he was German, he lived at the outcamp. Then there was Fred Stream, by jingoes, there was a few kids that belonged to him.

Aah, that colour business is a funny thing. Our colour goes away. You mix us with the white man, and pretty soon, you got no blackfellas left. Some of these whitefellas you see walkin' around, they really black underneath. You see, you never can tell. I'm old now, and look at me, look at the skin on my arms and legs, just look! It's goin' white. I used to be a lot darker than I am now. I don't know what's happened. Maybe it's the white blood takin' over, or the medicine they gave me in hospital, I don't know.

The big house on Corunna was built by the natives. They all worked together, building this and building that. If it wasn't for the natives, nothing would get done. They made the station, Drake-Brockmans didn't do it on their own.

At the back of the homestead was a big, deep hole with whitewash in it. It was thick and greasy, you could cut it with a knife. Us kids used to mix the whitewash with water and make it like a paint. Then we'd put it all over us and play corroborees every Saturday afternoon. We mixed the red sand with water and painted that on, too. By the time we finished, you didn't know what colour we were.

I 'member the kitchen on Corunna. There was a tiny little window where the blackfellas had to line up for tucker. My mother never liked doin' that. We got a bit of tea, flour and meat, that was all. They always rang a bell when they was ready for us to come. Why do white people like ringin' bells so much?

Every morning, they woke us up with a bell. It was only 'bout five o'clock, could have been earlier. We all slept down in the camp, a good way from the main house. Every morning, someone would light a lamp, walk down into the gully and ring a bell. When I was very little, I used to get frightened. I thought it was the devil-devil come to get me.

There was a tennis court on Corunna. Can you 'magine that? I think they thought they were royalty, puttin' in a tennis court. That's an Englishman's game. They painted it with whitewash, but it didn't stay white for long, I can tell you. I had a go at hitting the ball, once. I gave up after that, it was a silly game.

I saw plenty of willy-willies up there and cyclones, too. By jingoes, a cyclone is a terrible thing! When one was coming, my mother hid me. I wasn't allowed to move. She was worried I might get taken away by the wind. I was only small. I 'member one time we hid in the kitchen. When my mother wasn't looking, I sneaked up to the window and peeked out. You should have seen it! There was men's hats, spinifex, empty tanks, everything blowin' everywhere. It's a funny thing, but those old tanks always ended up settlin' on the tennis court.

There was a food store on Corunna. It had tin walls, tin

roof and a tiny window near the top covered with flywire. You wouldn't believe the food they had in there, sacks of apricots, potatoes, tobacco, everything. It makes my mouth water just thinkin' about it. When it was siesta time, the other kids used to lift me up and poke me through the window. I'd drop down inside as quiet as a mouse. Then I'd pick up food and throw it out the window. If they heard someone coming, they'd cough, then run away. I'd hide behind the sacks of potatoes and wait for them to come back for me. I had a good feed on those days.

The people were really hungry sometimes, poor things. They didn't get enough, you see. And they worked hard. You had to work hard, if you didn't, then they called the police in to make you work hard. When things was like that, one of the men would put me through the window again. I suppose I should feel bad about stealin' that food. Hunger is a terrible thing.

Aah, you see, the native is different to the white man. He wouldn't let a dog go without his tea.

Of course, the men all wanted their tobacco as well. The white man called it Nigger Twist. It was a twist like a licorice, only thicker. It's terrible, when you think about it, callin' something like that Nigger Twist. I mean, we all called it that because we thought that was its name.

Sometimes, we'd pinch the eggs the chooks laid in the hay shed. Aah, that old hay shed, it's kept a lot of secrets. There was plenty of stockmen up North then, and they all wanted girls. We'd be hearin' all this noise in the hay shed, the hay'd be goin' up and down, the hens'd be cluckin', the roosters crowin'. Then, by and by, out would come a stockman and one of the girls. They'd be all covered in hay. 'We just bin lookin' for eggs,' they'd say.

There was a government ration we used to get now and then. It was a blanket, we all called it a flag blanket, it had the crown of Queen Victoria on it. Can you imagine that? We used to laugh about that. You see, we was wrappin' ourselves in royalty. Then there was a mirror and a comb, a cake of soap and a couple of big spotted handkerchiefs. Sometimes, the men were lucky and got a shirt.

I 'member my mother showin' me a picture of a white woman, she was all fancied up in a long, white dress. 'Ooh, Daisy,' she said, 'if only I could have a dress like that.' All the native women wanted to look like the white women, with fancy hairdos and fancy dresses.

Later, my mother learnt to sew, she was very clever. She could draw anything, she loved drawing. She drew pictures in the sand for me all the time. Beautiful pictures. Maybe that's where you get it from, Sally.

We were cunning when we were kids. There was a big water trough on Corunna, it was used for the animals, even the camels had a drink from it. Mrs Stone always warned us not to muck around in the trough. We'd wait till she was sleeping, then we'd sneak down to the garden and dive in the trough. It was slimy and there was a lot of goona* in the water, but we didn't care. I 'member holding my breath and swimming under the water. I looked up and I could see the faces of all the animals lookin' down at me as if to say, 'What are you doin' in our water, child?'

They had a good cook on Corunna for a while, Mrs Quigley. She was a white woman, a good woman. She had a little girl called Queenie and it was my job to look out for her. We were 'bout the same age, ooh, we had good times! We'd laugh and giggle at anythin'. Giggling gerties—that's what Queenie's mother used to call us.

I taught Queenie all about the bush. We'd go out after a big rain. Sometimes, the rain was so heavy up North, it hurt when it hit you. That's the kind of rain you get in the wet. One day, the place would be desert, the next day, green everywhere. Green and gold, beautiful, really. I'd take Queenie out into the bush and we'd watch a little seed grow. 'Look now,' I'd say to Queenie, 'it's getting bigger.' By the time we finished lookin', that seed would be half an inch long.

In the evenings, I liked to sit and watch the kangaroos and other animals come down and drink at the trough. The

* *goona* — faeces.

crows and the birds would have a drink, too. I just liked to sit and watch them all. Course, you know, Corunna has blue hills all round it. They always looked soft that time of night. Sometimes, my mother would sit and watch, too. We knew how to count our blessings, then.

I was a hard worker on Corunna. I been a hard worker all my life. When I was little, I picked the grubs off the caulies and cabbages at the back of the garden. I got a boiled sweet for that. The blackfellas weren't allowed to pick any vegetables from the garden. You got a whipping if you were caught. Old Pompee, he used to sneak us tomatoes. And so he should have, he was eatin' them himself.

We all loved the orphaned lambs. We fed them with a bottle with a turkey feather stuck in it. There was one lamb I fed, dear little thing she was, she was blind. She kept bumpin' into the fence and the other lambs. Poor thing. I was so upset I told cook about it and she told me this story.

'You know, Daisy, when I was a young child in Sydney, I had very bad eyesight. One day, an old lady came to visit us and she asked my mother if she could have a go at curing me. Mother said yes. They sat down and put a single grain of sugar in each eye. Ooh, it hurt! I cried and cried, but pretty soon, I could see. I'll give you some sugar, you try that with your lamb.'

I did what she said, and pretty soon, that lamb's eyes were watering all over the place. Next thing I knew, it was runnin' around like all the other lambs, not bumpin' into anything. She was a wise woman, that cook.

There was a creek that cut across Corunna in the wet. We loved swimming in it and catching fish. They were like sardines, we threw them on the hot ashes and then gobbled them up.

All sorts of wild fruit grew along the creek. There was a prickly tree with fruit like an orange, but with lots of big seeds in it. You could suck the seeds. Then there was another one shaped like a banana, that was full of seeds, too. You ate the flesh and spat out the seeds. There was another prickly tree that had yellow flowers like a wattle, wild beans grew off that tree. When they swelled up, we picked them and threw them in the ashes. They were good.

The best one of all was like a gooseberry bush. Aah, if you could find a patch of that, you just stayed there and ate. You could smell those a good way away, they smell like a ripe rockmelon. We'd sniff and say, 'Aah, something ripe in there somewhere.' We'd lift up all the bushes looking for them, they were only tiny. When we found them, we'd say, 'Hmmmn, mingimullas, good old mingimullas.' I never tasted fruit like those mingimullas. They had soft green leaves like a flannel, ooh, they were good to eat.

There was another tree we used to get gum from to chew. It grew on little white sticks. We'd collect it and keep it in a tin. It went hard, like boiled lollies.

Rosie and I were naughty. We'd pinch wild ducks' eggs and break up their nests. And we'd dig holes to get lizards' eggs. We could tell where the lizards had covered up their eggs. We'd dig them all out, get the eggs and bust them. Those poor creatures. They never harmed us and there we were, breakin' up their eggs. We're all God's creatures, after all.

Rosie and I used to catch birds, too. We'd get a bit of wire netting and make a cage, then we'd take it down the creek and throw wheat around. We kept the cage a little bit lifted up and we tied a long bit of string to the wood underneath. You should have seen all the cockies, they loved wheat. When there was a big mob of them, we'd pull the string, down would come the cage and we'd have them trapped. Trouble was, we couldn't do anything with them, they kept biting us. In the end, we let them go.

When I got older, my jobs on Corunna changed. They started me working at the main house, sweeping the verandahs, emptying the toilets, scrubbing the tables and pots and pans and the floor. In those days, you scrubbed everything. In the mornings, I had to clean the hurricane lamps, then help in the kitchen.

There were always poisonous snakes hiding in the dark

corners of the kitchen. You couldn't see them, but you could hear them. *Sssss, ssssss, ssssss*, they went. Just like that. We cornered them and killed them with sticks.

Once I was working up the main house, I wasn't allowed down in the camp. If I had've known that, I'd have stayed where I was. I couldn't sleep with my mother now and I wasn't allowed to play with my old friends.

That was the worst thing about working at the main house, not seeing my mother every day. I knew she missed me. She would walk up from the camp and call, 'Daisy, Daisy,' just like that. I couldn't talk to her, I had too much work to do. It was hard for me, then. I had to sneak away just to see my own family and friends. They were camp natives, I was a house native.

Now, I had to sleep on the homestead verandah. Some nights, it was real cold, one blanket was too thin. On nights like that, the natives used to bring wool from the shearing shed and lay that beneath them.

I didn't mind sleeping on the verandah in summer because I slept near the old cooler. It was as big as a fireplace, they kept butter and milk in it. I'd wait till everyone was asleep, then I'd sneak into the cooler and pinch some butter. I loved it, but I was never allowed to have any.

Seems like I was always getting into trouble over food. I 'member once, Nell asked me to take an apple-pie to the house farther out on the station. Nell's real name was Eleanor, but everyone called her Nell. She was Howden Drake-Brockman's first white wife. Anyway, I kept walkin' and walkin' and smellin' that pie. Ooh, it smelled good. I couldn't stand it any longer, I hid in a gully and dug out a bit of pie with my fingers. It was beautiful. I squashed the pie together and tried to make out like it was all there. Hmmmnnn, that was good tucker, I said to myself as I walked on.

When I gave the pie to Mrs Stone, I had to give her a note that Nell had sent as well. If I had have known what was in that note, I'd have thrown it away. It said, if any part of this pie is missing, send the note back and I will punish her. Mrs

Stone looked at the note, then she looked at the pie, then she said, 'Give this note back when you go.' I did. And, sure enough, I got whipped with the bullocks' cane again.

Nell was a cruel woman, she had a hard heart. When she wasn't whippin' us girls with the bullocks' cane for not workin' hard enough, she was hittin' us over the head. She didn't like natives. If one of us was in her way and we didn't move real quick, she'd give us a real hard thump over the head, just like that. Ooh, it hurt! White people are great ones for thumpin' you on the head, aren't they? We was only kids.

Aah, but they were good old days, then. When they took me from the station, I never seen days like that ever again.

They told my mother I was goin' to get educated. They told all the people I was goin' to school. I thought it'd be good, goin' to school. I thought I'd be somebody real important. My mother wanted me to learn to read and write like white people. Then she wanted me to come back and teach her. There was a lot of the older people interested in learnin' how to read and write, then.

Why did they tell my mother that lie? Why do white people tell so many lies? I got nothin' out of their promises. My mother wouldn't have let me go just to work. They should have told my mother the truth. She thought I was coming back.

When I left, I was cryin', all the people were cryin', my mother was cryin' and beatin' her head. Lily was cryin'. I called, 'Mum, Mum, Mum!' She said, 'Don't forget me, Talahue!'

They all thought I was coming back. I thought I'd only be gone a little while. I could hear their wailing for miles and miles.

'Talahue! Talahue!' They were singin' out my name, over and over. I couldn't stop cryin'. I kept callin', 'Mum! Mum!'

Ivanhoe

I must have been 'bout fourteen or fifteen when they took me from Corunna. Now I was with Howden's second wife, Alice. Nell had died and he'd married again. First day in Perth, I had to tidy the garden, pick up leaves and sweep the verandahs. Later on, I used an old scythe to cut the grass. All the time, I kept wonderin' when they were goin' to send me to school. I saw some white kids goin' to school, but not me. I never asked them why they didn't send me, I was too 'shamed.

Funny how I was the only half-caste they took with them from Corunna. Maybe Howden took me 'cause I was his daughter, I don't know. I kept thinkin' of my poor old mother and how she thought I was gettin' educated. I wanted to tell her what had happened. I wanted to tell her all I was doin' was workin'. I wasn't gettin' no education. How could I tell her, when I couldn't write? And I had no one to write for me.

It wasn't the first time I'd been in Perth. I'd been there before with the first wife, Nell. Then I'd had to look after Jack and Betty, they were the children. I was only a kid myself. I was 'bout ten and Jack was 'bout six, I can't remember how old Betty was. We was all kids, but I had to do the work.

Aah, Nell was a hard woman. She was hard on her own kids, too. She bossed Howden around. He didn't step out of line with Nell around. When I was in Perth with her, she didn't even give me a place to sleep. I had to find my own place. There was a big, empty trunk on the verandah of the house. I climbed in there at night. At least it kept me out of the wind.

You see, I went to Perth with Nell, and I came back. My mother would be thinkin' I'd come back this time, too. She'd be thinkin' it was like before, but it wasn't. They just wanted me to work.

We moved into Ivanhoe, a big house on the banks of the Swan River in Claremont. I was lookin' after the children again, there was Jack and Betty, Judy, June and Dick, I was supposed to be their nanny. I had to play with them, dress them, feed them and put them to bed at night. I had other chores to do as well. I never blamed the children, it wasn't their fault I had to work so hard. I felt sorry for them.

At night, I used to lie in bed and think about my people. I could see their campfire and their faces. I could see my mother's face and Lily's. I really missed them. I cried myself to sleep every night. Sometimes, in my dreams, I'd hear them wailing, 'Talahue! Talahue!' and I'd wake up, calling 'Mum! Mum!' You see, I needed my people, they made me feel important. I belonged to them. I thought 'bout the animals, too. The kangaroos and birds. I missed all of them.

Alice kept tellin' me, 'We're family now, Daisy.'

Thing is, they wasn't my family. They were white, they'd grow up and go to school one day. I was black, I was a servant. How can they be your family?

The only friend I had then was Queenie's mother, Mrs Quigley. She was housekeeping for the Cruikshanks in Claremont. I used to sneak over and visit her whenever I could. She understood the North, she knew how hard it was for me. She never said much, but I knew she understood. I never stayed with her long. I was worried they'd notice I was missing. Aah, Queenie's mother was a kind woman. Sometimes, she'd tell me something funny to cheer me up.

I did all the work at Ivanhoe. The cleaning, the washing, the ironing. There wasn't nothing I didn't do. From when I got up in the morning till when I went to sleep at night, I worked. That's all I did really, work and sleep.

By jingoes, washing was hard work in those days. The old laundry was about twenty yards from the house and the troughs were always filled with dirty washing. They'd throw everything down from the balcony onto the grass, I'd collect it up, take it to the laundry and wash it. Sometimes I thought I'd never finish stokin' up that copper, washin' this and washin' that. Course, everything was starched in those days. Sheets, pillowcases, serviettes, tablecloths, they was all starched. I even had to iron the sheets. Isn't that silly, you only goin' to lay on them.

The house had to be spotless. I scrubbed, dusted and polished. There was the floors, the staircase, the ballroom. It all had to be done.

Soon, I was the cook, too. Mind you, I was a good cook. I didn't cook no rubbish. Aah, white people, they got some funny tastes. Fussy, fussy, aaah, they fussy. I 'member I had to serve the toast on a silver tray. I had to crush the edges of each triangle with a knife. Course, you never left the crusts on sandwiches, that was bad manners. Funny, isn't it? I mean, it's all bread, after all.

I had my dinner in the kitchen. I never ate with the family. When they rang the bell, I knew they wanted me. After dinner, I'd clear up, wash up, dry up and put it all away. Then, next morning, it'd start all over again. You see, it's no use them sayin' I was one of the family, 'cause I wasn't. I was their servant.

I 'member they used to have real fancy morning and afternoon teas. The family would sit on the lawn under a big, shady umbrella. I'd bring out the food and serve them. You know, I saw a picture like that on television. It was in England, they were all sittin' outside in their fancy clothes with servants waitin' on them. I thought, well fancy that, that's what I used to do.

I 'member the beautiful cups and saucers. They were very fine, you thought they'd break with you just lookin' at them. Ooh, I loved them. Some of them were so fine, they were like a seashell, you could see through them. I only ever had a tin mug. I promised myself one day I would have a nice cup and saucer. That's why, whenever my grandchildren said, 'What do you want for your birthday?' I always told them a cup and saucer.

In those days, the Drake-Brockmans were real upper class. They had money and people listened to them. Aah, the parties they had. I never seen such parties. The ladies' dresses were pretty and fancy. I always thought of my mother when I saw their dresses. How she would have loved one.

Arthur

I never liked Perth much, then. I was too scared. I was shy, too. I couldn't talk to strangers. People looked at you funny 'cause you were black. I kept my eyes down. Maybe some of those white people thought the cat got my tongue, I don't know. I'm not sayin' they was all bad. Some of them was nice. You get nice people anywhere. Trouble is, you get the other ones as well. 'Cause you're black, they treat you like dirt. You see, in those days, we was owned, like a cow or a horse. I even heard some people say we not the same as whites. That's not true, we all God's children.

Course, when the white people wanted something, they didn't pretend you wasn't there, they 'spected you to come runnin' quick smart. That's all I did sometimes, run in and out. Someone was always ringin' that bell.

I'm 'shamed of myself, now. I feel 'shamed for some of the things I done. I wanted to be white, you see. I'd lie in bed at night and think if God could make me white, it'd be the best thing. Then I could get on in the world, make somethin' of myself. Fancy, me thinkin' that. What was wrong with my own people?

In those days, it was considered a privilege for a white man to want you, but if you had his children, you weren't allowed to keep them. You was only allowed to keep the black ones. They took the white ones off you 'cause you weren't considered fit to raise a child with white blood. I tell you, it made a wedge between the people. Some of the black men felt real low, and some of the native girls with a bit of white in them wouldn't look at a black man. There I was, stuck in the middle. Too black for the whites and too white for the blacks.

I 'member when more native girls came into Perth as servants, they all looked to Nellie and me. Nellie worked for the Courthope family, they were good to her. The other native girls thought we were better than them because we had some white in us.

It was a big thing if you could get a white man to marry

you. A lot of native people who were light passed themselves off as white, then. You couldn't blame them, it was very hard to live as a native. One of my friends married a Slav. I think that's how you call it. He was a foreigner, anyway. She came to say goodbye to me and Nellie. We was all cryin'. She'd promised her husband never to talk or mix with any natives again. We didn't blame her, we understood. He wouldn't have married her, otherwise.

Nellie was from Lyndon Station, she was the daughter of the station manager, Mr Hack, but he never owned her. The Courthope family got her to be a servant in their house. Nellie was lucky, because she got treated kindly. She worked very hard like me, but they was good to her. She had a lovely room.

Aah, she was a laugh, that Nellie. She always wanted to be white. All those baths in that hydrogen peroxide and dyin' her hair red. Sometimes, she'd forget to take those baths and then she'd go black again.

You know, I been thinkin' a lot 'bout this. People mustn't say the blackfella has never done anythin' good for this country. I knew this black woman, Tillie, she was a servant and she joined the Salvation Army. She led a real good life, helpin' her own people when she could. She made me feel bad for not goin' to church on Sunday night when she could take me. I didn't like church. People there didn't understand what it was like for the natives.

I 'member the minister at Christ Church started up a sewing circle for all the native servants. We had to go down there and he'd give us a talk, then we'd sew. One time, he went on and on, tellin' us how we must save ourselves for marriage. It was very embarrassing, we couldn't look at him. Most of us had already been taken by white men. We felt really 'shamed. One day, we were sittin' in the garden sewing when boys from Christ Church Grammar School came past. They laughed at us and called us awful names. Then they threw pebbles at us. I never went back there, I was too 'shamed to say why.

We had no protection when we was in service. I know a lot

of native servants had kids to white men because they was forced. Makes you want to cry to think how black women have been treated in this country. It's a terrible thing.

Aah, white people make you laugh the way they beat the native to teach him not to steal. What about their own kids? I seen white kids do worse than that and no one touches them. They say, he's sowin' his oats or that kid got the devil in him, but they not belted. Poor old blackfella do the same thing, they say 'You niggers don't know right from wrong' and they whip you! I tell you, this is a white man's world.

The only one of my own people I had in Perth was Arthur. Now if I been livin' with my big brother Arthur, he'd have protected me. He was a strong man. I 'member I was standin' in the kitchen cooking when I heard this knock. I turned around and there's this big native lookin' through the flywire.

'Is that you, Daisy?' he said.

'Who are you?' I asked.

'Aah, you not Daisy,' he said. 'She had real fair hair. Come on Missus, you tell me where Daisy is.'

'What you want her for?' I wasn't gunna let him in the door.

'That's for me to know and you to find out,' he said. Aah, I thought, he's got tickets on himself.

'You listen here,' I growled at him. 'We don't like strange blackfellas hangin' round here. You better get goin' before the mistress comes home. She'll take a stick to you.' I was tryin' to frighten him.

'Don't you go gettin' uppity with me, Missus,' he said. 'Thinkin' you're better just 'cause you work for white people. I got every right to be lookin' for my little sister Daisy. I want her to know she's got a brother who's gettin' on in the world.'

I couldn't believe it. Can you 'magine that? This big, ugly blackfella was my brother.

'You Arthur?'

'Now how did you come by my name?'

'You cheeky devil,' I said, 'I'm your sister Daisy.' He just stood there. 'Well, come in,' I said. I didn't want him out there clutterin' up the verandah.

'What did you dye your hair for?' he asked. 'You was the only one of us with blonde hair.'

'Don't be stupid. This is the colour of my hair!'

Cheeky devil, he pulled my hair. Maybe he 'spected the colour to come off. Maybe he thought I put boot polish on my hair, I don't know. 'By gee, you a devil!' I told him. I should have known he was my brother, I was fightin' with him, wasn't I?

It wasn't so bad after that. Arthur would come and take me out. Sometimes, he even took me in a car. Can you 'magine that? All us natives drivin' round Perth in a real car? Aah, he thought he was somebody, that Arthur. All the girls wanted him, then. He was the only blackfella they knew with a bit of money in his pocket.

We always went to see the horses. We loved horses. One time, he took me to the Show. By gee, he was tough. He'd take on anyone. I said to him, 'Don't you get into no fights when you're out with me. It's not proper. I'll give you what for if you get silly.' You see, he loved showin' off, lived for it.

If he wouldn't settle down, I'd say, 'You just a silly old blackfella.'

One day, he said to me, 'Daisy, don't talk to me like that when we out. I'm your brother, you got to show me some respect.' Hmmph, the way he carried on you'd think he was a white man.

When he didn't come, I missed him. We always had a good laugh together. Sometimes he was too busy puttin' crops in to bother with me. He was a hard worker, he did it all on his own.

When he couldn't come to see me, he'd write. I felt real important, gettin' a letter with my name on it. Trouble was, I couldn't read. I couldn't have nothin' private 'cause I always had to get someone to read it for me.

Aah, he was a clever man. We had fights all the time, but I was proud of that man.

Gladdie

I hadn't seen Arthur for a long time when I had Gladdie.

Before I had Gladdie, I was carryin' another child, but I wasn't allowed to keep it. That was the way of it, then. They took our children one way or another. I never told anyone I was carryin' Gladdie.

Now how this all came about, that's my business, I'll only tell a little. Everyone knew who the father was, but they all pretended they didn't know. Aah, they knew, they knew. You didn't talk 'bout things, then, you hid the truth.

Alice bought me a cane pram to wheel Gladdie in. She gave Gladdie a doll. I kept Gladdie with me in my room.

Howden died not long after she was born. When I came home from hospital, he said, 'Bring her here, let me hold her.' He wanted to nurse Gladdie before he died.

After he died, I never had time for anything. I had Gladdie and the other children to look after. There were times when Gladdie ate so much she 'minded me of the little baby pigs runnin' round the station. It was hard for me with her. Sometimes, she'd be cryin', cryin', and I couldn't go to her. I had too much work to do.

When Arthur saw her, he thought she was beautiful. Strange, isn't it, at one time, I was goin' to live with Arthur. It was before I had Gladdie, the Drake-Brockmans said they didn't want me any more. Then they changed their minds. Arthur told me he had a real nice whitefella for me to marry. After Gladdie was born, Arthur wanted us both to go with him. I wasn't allowed to go anywhere. I had to have permission and they wouldn't let me go. I knew Arthur would have been good to Gladdie, she had him by the heartstrings. When it came to little ones, Arthur was real tender-hearted.

When Gladdie was about three years old, they took her from me. I'd been 'spectin' it. Alice told me Gladdie needed an education, so they put her in Parkerville Children's Home. What could I do? I was too frightened to say anythin'. I wanted to keep her with me, she was all I had, but they didn't want her there. Alice said she cost too much to feed, said I was ungrateful. She was wantin' me to give up my own flesh and blood and still be grateful. Aren't black people allowed to have feelings?

I cried and cried when Alice took her away. Gladdie was too young to understand, she thought she was comin' back. She thought it was a picnic she was goin' on. I ran down to the wild bamboo near the river to hide and I cried and cried and cried. How can a mother lose a child like that? How could Alice do that to me? I thought of my poor old mother then, they took her Arthur from her, and then they took me. She was broken-hearted, God bless her.

When Gladdie was in Parkerville, I tried to get up there as often as I could, but it was a long way and I had no money. When I did get paid, Alice was always takin' money out that she said I owed her. It was a hard life. I always got Gladdie something nice to eat when I went up.

Parkerville wasn't a bad place, there was plenty of kids for her to play with and there was bush everywhere. I knew she'd love the bush. I used to take her for a bit of a walk, show her the birds and animals like. She was always real glad to see me. I knew she didn't want to stay there, but what could I do? It wasn't like I had a place of my own. It wasn't like I had any say over my own life.

It was during the thirties that they told Gladdie I might die. My cousin Helen Bunda was real sick. They asked me to give blood for her. I said yes. She belonged to me, I had to give blood, but I was real scared.

You never know what doctors are goin' to do to you. They lost the first lot of blood they took, so they took some more. I was so weak I couldn't lift my head. I think I turned white with all the blood they took from me.

Helen died and I heard the doctors say, 'Doesn't matter, she was only a native.' Then, they looked at me and the nurse said, 'I think this one's going, too.' You see, they treat you just like an animal. Alice came and got me, she was very cross. She took me back to Ivanhoe and nursed me. She was a good bush nurse.

They brought Gladdie down from Parkerville to say goodbye to me. She looked real frightened when she saw me. I tricked all of them, I didn't die, after all. Pretty soon, I was up and doin' all the work again. That's the last time I give blood.

Helen had been a good old cousin. She was mean, though. She'd walk five miles to save a ha'penny. She was good with her hands. No one could sew the way she could. She'd had a hard life, work, work, work. They'd sent her to Moore River. I don't know if you ever heard of it. She had three kids there and was made to leave them there and go back to service. I think all those kids died. It was a terrible place. No one wanted to go to Moore River, no fear. Poor old Bunda. I knew how she felt, it was the same with all of us.

When she died, I thought her things would come to me, I was her family. Turned out I got nothin', not a penny. The white family that she was workin' for got it all. They said she made a will leavin' it to them. Bunda didn't know nothin' 'bout will-makin'. I don't think she could even write much. That family even asked me to give back the brooch she'd given me. The cheek of it. Bunda belonged to me, she'd given it me before she died and they asked for it back. 'That brooch doesn't belong to you now, Daisy,' they said, 'it's ours now, you got to hand it over.' I felt very bitter 'bout that. Right inside my heart, I felt bitter.

Arthur finally got married in the thirties and I lost track of him. The Depression was on and I knew he'd be havin' trouble makin' ends meet. It was just as well Gladdie and I hadn't gone with him. We'd only be two more mouths to feed. He worked real hard, did anythin' to put food on the table. I think he lost his farm in the Depression. Those white people at Mucka, they were always after his farm. Funny, isn't it, the white man's had land rights for years, and we not allowed to have any. Aah, this is a funny world.

Couple of times, Arthur saw Gladdie at Parkerville. He had a real soft spot for her. Then he got too busy with his own family to see her. I think she missed him. She loved visitors.

The thirties was hard for everyone. You never threw anythin' away, there was always someone who could use it. It broke my heart to see men standin' round for food. Not just black men, white ones, too. If I knew someone who was hungry, I'd give them food. I gave away some of my clothes and shoes, whatever I could find. You can't be rotten to people when they in trouble, that's not the blackfella's way.

When Gladdie was 'bout fourteen, she left Parkerville. She'd been with me for holidays at Ivanhoe, and when I took her back, she didn't want to stay. You see, she found out she was havin' this new House Mother and she was a cruel woman. Gladdie was real frightened. I said to them, 'Can she come with me, she's almost grown-up now.'

They asked Gladdie if she wanted to leave Parkerville and she said, 'Too right!'

I took her back to Ivanhoe with me. I thought she could stay in my room, but after two days, Alice said, 'Look Daisy, you can't keep her here. You'll have to find somewhere else for her to go.' I was real upset 'bout that.

They'd told me to leave before, reckoned they couldn't afford me. I had to go and work for Mrs Morgan. Then, a few years later, Alice begged me to come back. She said it was for good, that Ivanhoe was my home. I thought it would be Gladdie's, too. Aah, you see, the promises of a wealthy family are worth nothin'.

I found a family to take Gladdie in. They were religious people and they often took girls in. I knew they'd be good to her. She was real upset, she couldn't understand why they didn't want her at Ivanhoe.

One day, the Hewitts, that was their name, said they couldn't trust Gladdie no more. 'She's been goin' to the pictures,' they said. 'Pictures are a sin.' They said they didn't want her bein' a bad influence on the other kids. They packed her bags and said I had to take her.

I was livin' in my own place by then. Alice had kicked me out again. Aah, I was silly to believe her. She owed me back wages, got me to work for nothing, then kicked me out. I was just used up. I been workin' for that family all those years, right since I was a little child, and that's how I get treated. I left a good job to go back to Ivanhoe. I was silly. I should have known. When they didn't want Gladdie stayin' there, I should have known.

I reckon they wasted their money, it was all that high livin'. Everyone thought they was real important. Hmmph, I never seen any of their money. Howden, he promised Arthur and me money. He said he'd leave us some. Haa, that's how you get treated by rich people, real rotten. I think they get greedy, they live for the money. All Alice ever gave me was a couple of odds and ends and an old broom. After all those years, that was all I got.

I 'member there was this beautiful picture of Fremantle that Alice had. She was sendin' a lot of stuff to auction houses, then. You see, they was goin' to live in Sydney. I asked if I could have that picture, but they said it was goin' to auction. There was some other pictures I asked for, but they made a big bonfire and burnt them. I thought, well, I got wages now, I'll buy my own things. Some people you're better off without.

My new job was a cook in a restaurant. All the soldiers and sailors loved to come in, because we served good tucker and I gave them plenty. I never cook rubbish. By gee, they could eat. They all wanted second helpings. I felt sorry for them. Some of them were only kids. Goin' to war like that, it's not right.

I shared a house with a good woman. She liked Gladdie, she was good to her. Gladdie and I was livin' together for the first time. She was makin' new friends and so was I. Pretty soon, I was goin' to the trots and other places. I really loved the horses. I'm like Arthur, I got a tender spot for all God's creatures.

Gladdie left school and Alice got her a job as a florist. They didn't want to take her, because she was a native. But they were pleased they took her in the end, because everyone loved Gladdie.

Now you'd be thinkin' that, after all those years apart, we'd get on real good. Well, we didn't. Gladdie liked to do things her way and I liked to do things my way. We was fightin' and fightin'. By jingoes, we had some rows.

Gladdie was silly in those days, always wantin' to know her future. She didn't know what she was meddlin' with. You leave the spirits alone. You mess with them, you get burnt. She had her palm read, her tea-leaves read, I don't know what she didn't get read. I never went with her to any of these fortune-tellers. They give you a funny feeling inside. Blackfellas know all about spirits. We brought up with them. That's where the white man's stupid. He only believes what he can see. He needs to get educated. He's only livin' half a life.

Gladdie didn't like some of my friends and I didn't like some of hers. Now maybe she was right 'bout some of my friends and maybe she wasn't, but I think it's true that you don't get many real true friends in this life. There's not many that'll stand by you in trouble. They the rare ones. Gladdie was always tellin' me I was too suspicious. She said I didn't trust her. Maybe I didn't. Maybe it was the men I didn't trust. Gladdie was innocent. She knew nothin' 'bout life. She didn't know what could happen.

One day, she just went off and got married. She was only twenty-one. I s'pose she didn't tell me because she knew I didn't like Bill. He was a drinker. I never liked men who were drinkers. What was she goin' and gettin' married for, anyway? She should have been home, lookin' after her mother.

Well, there's no use cryin' over spilt milk. What's done is done. They got a State Housing place in Mulberry Farm, that's near Beaconsfield. It wasn't a bad little place. I used to visit them, take them a bit of meat. There were some poor families there. Sometimes I gave them meat, too. I don't 'member anyone sayin' thank you. Still, you can't let people go hungry.

'By Gee, It'd Be Good'

Pretty soon, I was havin' grandchildren. You was the first, Sally, but you was so sick. Jilly wasn't like you, she was real healthy and she wasn't naughty.

I felt real sorry for Gladdie. She didn't realise how bad Bill was when she married him. He kept disappearing. She was worried sick. She never knew where he was. It was the grog, you see. The grog got the better of him. I'm not sayin' he was a bad man. He had a hard time during the war.

When Gladdie was carrying Billy, she got polio. There wasn't one family in Mulberry Farm that wasn't touched with polio. It was a terrible thing. I was worried you kids might get sick, too. That's when I moved in. Gladdie couldn't walk, she was stuck in bed. There was no one to look after you and Jilly. Bill didn't like me there. He was jealous. He wanted Gladdie to himself. What could she do? She needed someone to mind the kids. He was no good around the house.

Now, I tell you something, Sal, this is a sacred thing, so I better speak quiet. I helped your mother with that polio. You see, our family's always had powers that way. I don't want to say no more. Some things I'm tellin' you 'cause I won't be here much longer. That's something you should know.

Gladdie and Bill was offered a house in Manning. It was made from bricks and bigger than the one we was livin' in. Billy was a baby then, and Gladdie was over the polio. I liked the new place. There was bush everywhere. You couldn't see nothin' but bush, and it was near the river. Aah, the birds and the wildlife, it was wonderful. Trouble was, it stank at night. We was near the swamp. That night air was bad for you, Sally. It made you sick. You should have been up North, you're no good in the cold.

Now, this is something I've told no one. You mightn't believe me. 'Member when we first moved there? Couple of nights, you came out on the back verandah and found Gladdie and me sittin' there, 'member we made you go away?

You was always in the wrong place at the wrong time. Well, we was listenin' to music. It was the blackfellas playin' their didgeridoos and singin' and laughin' down in the swamp. Your mother could hear it. I said to her one night, 'I'm goin' down there to tell those natives off. Who do they think they are, wakin' all the white people up?' That's when Gladdie told me. She said, 'Don't go down there, Mum, there's no one there, only bush.' You see, we was hearin' the people from long ago. Our people who used to live here before the white man came. Funny, they stopped playin' after your father died. I think now they was protectin' us. You see, the blackfella knows all 'bout spirits.

It was hard for us with Bill. He couldn't get away from the grog. We had no money. Grog's a curse. Gladdie and I couldn't help him.

There was rows all the time with Bill. You know all 'bout that, so I'll say no more. Just between you and me, Bill's parents didn't like natives. They said things 'bout Gladdie behind her back. They said she wasn't good enough for Bill. They blamed her for his troubles. It wasn't her fault, she was doin' the best she could.

'Member we used to keep you kids out the way? We didn't want to upset him. Any little thing upset him. We was frightened of what he might do.

I never told anyone this, but you was close to your father, you knew what he was like. I never even told your mother. I just kept it to myself. When Gladdie wasn't around, Bill used to call me a bloody nigger. I know he had a bad time in the war, but he shouldn't have called me that. No one should call anyone that. I kept quiet 'bout it 'cause I didn't want to cause trouble, but it hurt me real bad to hear him say that.

He wasn't a bad man, he was just very sick. When he died, I'd been expectin' it. I had that feelin' inside he might be goin' soon. I think Gladdie knew, too. Course, you know little David found the body. Poor little bloke, he was only 'bout two, then. He thought Bill was asleep, he kept tryin' to wake him up.

David and you are a lot alike, Sal. He wasn't naughty like

you, mind, but you both got a feel for the spiritual side of things.

I think Bill knew he was goin' to die. He made his peace. He knew where he was goin'. 'Member he played footy with Billy and David? Aah, it was a sad time. If it hadn't been for the grog and the war, he'd have been a different man. A good man.

Bill's parents were mongrels after he died. They didn't help Gladdie. They wasn't interested in you kids. We had no money, nothin' left to sell. We didn't know what we was goin' to do, we was desperate. Gladdie wrote to the Drake-Brockmans in Sydney to see if they could give us a loan. They said they was broke, too.

Lois was good to your mother, then. She gave us some money. Frank Potter was good to us.

We was worried 'bout you kids. We thought the government might come and get you. They didn't like people like us rearin' kids with white blood in them. Seems like no one took account of the black blood.

I tried to stay out the way after Bill died. Gladdie could pass for anythin'. You only had to look at me to see I was a native. We had to be careful. 'Tell them they're Indian,' I told her. 'You don't want them havin' a bad time.'

There was men interested in Gladdie, she was a beautiful woman. She didn't want no one. All she wanted was you kids. Good men are rare in this world.

Well, Sal, that's all I'm gunna tell ya. I don't want to talk no more. I got my secrets, I'll take them to the grave. Some things, I can't talk 'bout. Not even to you, my granddaughter. They for me to know. They not for you or your mother to know.

I'm glad I won't be here in body when you finish that book. I'm glad I'm goin'. You a stirrer, you gunna have a lot of talkin' to do. I can't stick up for myself, you see. It's better you do it. Look out for your mother, she's like me. Aah, you've always been naughty. I'm not frightened for you any more, Sal, you'll be protected. I think maybe this is a good thing you're doin'. I didn't want you to do it, mind. But I think, now, maybe it's a good thing. Could be it's time to tell. Time to tell what it's been like in this country.

I want you grandchildren to make something of yourselves. You all got brains. One of you could be Prime Minister, one day. I hope you'll never be 'shamed of me. When you see them old fellas sittin' in the dirt, remember that was me, once.

Aah, I'm tired of this world now. I want to get on to the next one. God's got a spot up there for me, I dunno what it's like. Probably a bit of bush, eh? What do you think? Old Arthur'll be waitin' for me. We can have a good old fight. I bet he's causin' trouble up there.

I feel real tired, now, Sal, the fight's gone out o' me. I got no strength left.

Now you asked me 'bout the future. That's a hard question. I got no education, how can I answer a question like that? You think I'm a fortune-teller, eh?

But I'll tell you what I'm wonderin'. I'm wonderin' if they'll give the blackfellas land. If it's one thing I've learnt in this world it's this, you can't trust the government. They'll give the blackfellas the dirt and the mining companies will get the gold. That's the way of it.

I don't like this word Land Rights, people are gettin' upset 'bout it. I dunno what this word means. I've heard it on the news.

You know what I think? The government and the white man must own up to their mistakes. There's been a lot of coverin' up. Maybe they want us all to die off so no one'll talk. No use you goin' on at me, Sal, you can't blame us old ones for not wantin' to talk. We too scared.

Well, I'm hopin' things will change one day. At least we not owned any more. I was owned by the Drake-Brockmans and the government and anyone who wanted to pay five shillings a year for me. Not much, is it? I know it's hard for you to understand, Sal. You different to me. I been scared all my life, too scared to speak out. Maybe if you'd have had my life, you'd be scared, too.

Aah, I can't really say what will happen. I s'pose it don't concern me no more.

As for my people, some of them are naughty, they drink too much. Grog's a curse, I've seen what it can do. They got to give it up. They got to show the white man what they made of.

Do you think we'll get some respect? I like to think the black man will get treated same as the white man one day. Be good, wouldn't it? By gee, it'd be good.

6

THE BIRD CALL

When Nan finished telling me her story, I was filled with conflicting emotions. I was happy for her because she felt she'd achieved something. It meant so much to be able to talk and to be believed. But I was sad for myself and my mother. Sad for all the things Nan felt she couldn't share.

One thing quite surprised me. Nan's voice had changed as she reminisced. She could speak perfect English when she wanted to, and usually did, only occasionally dropping the beginning or ending of a word. But in talking about the past, her language had changed. It was as though she was back there, reliving everything. It made me realise that at one stage in her life it must have been difficult for her to speak English, and therefore to express herself. This made me even more aware of how much we still didn't know. My mind went over and over her story; every word, every look. I knew there were great dark depths there, and I knew I would never plumb them.

I felt, for Mum's sake, I should make one last effort to find out about her sister. So a few nights later, when Nan and I were on our own, I said, 'There's something I want to ask you. I know you won't like it, but I have to ask. It's up to you whether you tell me anything or not.'

Nan grunted. 'Well, ask away.'

'Has Mum got a sister somewhere?'

She looked away quickly. There was silence, then, after a few seconds, a long, deep sigh.

When she finally turned to face me, her cheeks were wet. 'Don't you understand yet,' she said softly, 'there are some things I just can't talk 'bout.' Her hand touched her chest in that characteristic gesture that meant her heart was hurting. It wasn't her flesh-and-blood heart. It was the heart of her spirit. With that, she heaved herself up and went out to her room.

I went to bed with a face full of tears and a mind full of guilt. I was so insensitive, sometimes. I should have known better.

The early morning brought some peace. I would never ask her another thing about the past. And she hadn't extinguished my small shred of hope. She'd even admitted that she was pregnant before she had Mum. That was a big thing. For the moment, it would have to be enough. I stretched and shouted towards the ceiling, 'I'm not giving up, God. Not in a million years. If she's alive, I'll find her, and I expect you to help!'

One night later that week, Nan called me out to her room.

'What on earth are you doing?' I laughed when I found her with both arms raised in the air and her head completely covered by the man's singlet she was wearing.

'I'm stuck,' she muttered, 'get me out.' I pulled the singlet off and helped her undress. It had become a difficult task for her lately. Her arthritis was worse and cataracts now almost completely obscured her vision.

'Can you give me a rub?' she asked. 'The Vaseline's over there.' I picked up the jar, dobbed a big, greasy lump of it onto her back and began to rub. Nan loved Vaseline. Good for keeping your body cool and moist, she always told me. She had a lot of theories like that.

'Ooh, that's good, Sally,' she murmured. As I continued to rub, she let out a deep sigh and then said slowly, 'You know, Sal...all my life, I been treated rotten, real rotten. Nobody's cared if I've looked pretty. I been treated just like a beast of the field. And now, here I am...old. Just a dirty old blackfella.'

I don't know how long it was before I answered her. My heart felt cut in half. I could actually see a beast in a field. A work animal, nothing more.

'You're not to talk about yourself like that,' I replied finally in a controlled voice. 'You're my grandmother and I won't have you talk like that. The whole family loves you. We'd do anything for you.'

There was no reply. How hollow my words sounded. How empty and limited. Would anything I said ever help? I hoped that she sensed how deeply I felt. Words were unnecessary for that.

I helped her into her nightclothes. This was no mean feat, there were so many. It was well into winter now, and Nan was anxious about the cold. I pulled a clean man's singlet over her head, then a fleecy nightgown and a bedjacket. While she pulled a South Fremantle football beanie down over her head, I covered her feet with two pairs of woollen socks. After that, she wound two long scarves around her neck.

'Are you sure you'll be warm enough?' I asked sarcastically.

'I think you better help me into that cardigan,' she answered after a second's thought, 'better safe than sorry.'

Once that was on, I pulled back the rugs and she rolled in on top of her sheepskin. I passed her a hot-water bottle.

I smiled as I tucked her in. 'Do you want me to turn your heater on?' Often she had it going all night.

'I'll do without it, takes the oxygen out of the air.'

'Remember when we were kids and you used to put all that newspaper between your sheets to keep warm? We heard you every time you rolled over.'

'That's a good old standby, newspaper. Don't you ever forget it.' A pause. 'Sal, leave the light on tonight, it might help me sleep.'

'You usually have it off.'

'I know, but I can't sleep with it off, so I might as well try with it on.'

I had half-closed the door when she suddenly murmured, 'Aah, Sal, you're too good to me...'

'You're my grandmother,' I replied quietly, 'how do you expect me to treat you?'

She never answered. Her eyes were closed.

When Nan was getting ready to go home to Mum that weekend, she said, 'You'll keep what I told you safe, won't you?'

'Of course I will.'

'You see, Arthur's not the only one with a good story.'

'He sure isn't!'

'I'll be back on Monday, bring you some goodies. Here' — she squeezed my hand — 'buy the kids something.'

'Come on, Nan,' Mum called from the front porch, 'the dogs'll be hungry for their tea.'

'I'm coming,' Nan replied crossly. Then, turning to me, she whispered, 'She's never worried about the dogs' tea before.'

'Well, she hasn't got you to feed them now.'

'Do her good to do a bit of work for a change,' Nan chuckled. She loved being in a position of power over Mum. Whenever Mum growled at her or tried to hurry her along, she'd say, 'You speak to me like that again, Gladdie, and I'll move in with Sally for good. Then you'll be sorry.' Poor Mum couldn't win.

The weekend passed quickly. When Nan hadn't arrived at my place by ten o'clock Monday morning, I began to worry. The phone rang and I rushed to answer it.

'Sally?' It was Mum.

'What's wrong?'

'She's taken a sudden turn for the worse. The doctor says she can't be moved.'

'Is she conscious?'

'At the moment, she's slipping in and out.'
'I'm coming over.'
'Jill's coming, too.'

I hung up. It had come so suddenly. She'd been living with me for over six weeks. She hadn't seemed like someone who was dying.

From then on, Nan was confined to bed. Jill, Mum and I took four-hourly shifts so that she was never alone. Bill and David came when they could. And when Helen was off-duty, she also came and sat with Nan.

Poor Helen, Nan would go on and on about how useless doctors were. It was a sensitive area. No one had the courage to disagree with her.

One night, Jill and I sat watching Nan sleep. Jill whispered, 'Doesn't seem fair, does it?'

'How do you mean?'

'Well, we're only just coming to terms with everything, finding ourselves, what we really are. And now she's dying. She's our link with the past and she's going.' I couldn't look at Jill. She sighed. 'With Nan gone, we could pass for anything. Greek, Italian, Indian... What a joke. We wouldn't want to, now. It's too important. It'd be like she never existed. As though her life meant nothing, not even to her own family.'

'We're all changing. I know we don't talk about it, but it's there.'

'When this is over,' Jill said, 'I'm going to stand up and be counted.'

I felt very close to Jill then. We both stayed there quietly watching as Nan slept peacefully. It was a promise. A promise from our spirits to hers. We would never forget.

The atmosphere had been electric over the past week. We were all physically exhausted. Some days, we walked around not saying anything, other days, we joked about nothing at all. Every now and then, we fought. We all knew something more than Nan's body was dying. She was a symbol. Part of us was going, too. We couldn't explain it. It was a time none of us understood.

Things finally came to a head and Mum asked Ruth, my brother David's wife, if she would mind doing the nightshift. Ruth was a trained nursing aide, and had looked after many people with terminal illnesses. She'd wanted to help all along, but knew we were all very sensitive, so had refrained from intruding.

It was Ruth, more than anyone, who understood Nan's fear of going before she was ready. They had little talks about it, during which Ruth would reassure her. Nan and Ruth had conflicted in the past, they were both stubborn, but as Ruth nursed her so tenderly, she came to mean a great deal to Nan. It was lovely to hear Nan say, 'Where's my nursie, is she still here? What would I do without her, Sally, she's so good to me.'

By the time Nan had been bedridden well over a week, I began to worry she might have a slow, lingering death.

One night, I confided my fears to Ruth.

'Do you think we should pray?' Ruth suggested.

'I pray every night.'

'No, I mean with her. It might help her to let go.'

'It might be a good idea, we'd have to ask her, couldn't force anything on her.'

We moved close to Nan's bedside and clasped her hands.

'Nan,' Ruth said quietly, 'can you hear me?' Nan nodded. 'Sally wants to talk to you, Nan.'

I squeezed her hand and then said gently, 'Nan, we were wondering if you would like us to pray for you. We would ask God to take you quickly if you like. You know how Ruth's told you you won't go before you're ready? Well, that's true. We won't pray unless you want us to. It's up to you.'

Tears slowly slid from under her closed eyelids. She lay quietly for a few minutes, then squeezed both our hands and said firmly, 'Do it. Please do it.'

I looked at Ruth. 'You do it,' she said.

We bowed our heads. What was I going to say? I tightened my grip on Nan's hand, cleared my throat and said, 'God...you know this is about Nan. We really love her and we know you do, too. She's tired of this world now, she's ready to go. We know you've got a good place up there. A big, old gum tree where she can sit. Arthur's waiting for her, and the others. Please show your mercy and take Nan quickly.' When I finished, I couldn't see for tears in my eyes. Ruth was crying, too.

Nan squeezed both our hands then gently let go. Within a few minutes, she was asleep.

The Silver Chain sister visited that afternoon. As I saw her to the door, she said, 'Your grandmother's changed. I think she's decided to die.'

'She has,' I agreed. 'It won't be long now.'

She grasped my arm and looked at me with pity in her eyes.

'You're wrong, dear,' she said, 'I've seen this happen before, many, many times. They give up the will to live, but they don't die, because their bodies just won't let them. She has a very strong heart and a good pulse. It could be weeks.'

'That won't happen with her,' I replied confidently. 'She'll be gone soon.'

The sister shrugged her shoulders sympathetically. 'Don't count on it, dear, you'll only be disappointed. There'd be a chance if her pulse was weak, but it's not. I think you should face up to the fact that this could go on for quite a while.'

The following morning, my phone rang very early.

'Hello,' I said as I lifted the receiver.

'I heard the bird call.' It was Jill's voice.

'What bird call?'

'This morning, about five o'clock. I heard it, Sally. It was a weird sound, like a bird call, only it wasn't. It was something spiritual, something out of this world. I think she'll be going soon.'

After breakfast, I hurried over. There was an air of excitement about the place. The heaviness that we'd all been living under seemed to have suddenly lifted.

Mum was mystified about the bird call. I think she felt a little left out. Jill couldn't understand why Mum hadn't heard it, it'd been so loud and gone on and on.

When I walked into Nan's room, I couldn't believe my eyes. She didn't look sick any more. Her face was bright and she was propped up in bed, smiling. Something had definitely happened, but none of us knew what. Even Mum and Jill were happier and bustling around like their old selves.

'Nan, you look really good,' I said in surprise.

'Feel good, Sal.'

I just stood there, smiling. She seemed so contented. Almost as though she had a secret. I was desperate to ask her about the bird call, but I didn't know how. I sat by the bed and patted her hand.

Just then, Mum popped in. 'Doesn't she look well, Sally,' she said happily.

'Sure does.'

'Get me some toast, Gladdie,' Nan said cheekily, 'I'm hungry.' Mum rushed out with tears in her eyes.

'Nan,' I said slowly as she looked at me, 'you weren't frightened when you heard that call, were you?'

'Ooh, no,' she scoffed. 'It was the Aboriginal bird, Sally. God sent him to tell me I'm going home soon. Home to my own land and my own people. I got a good spot up there, they all waitin' for me.'

A lump formed in my throat so big I couldn't speak, let alone swallow.

Mum popped back in with tea and toast. ''Bout time,' Nan chuckled. She ate a little and then lay back. 'Think I'll sleep now,' she sighed.

We tiptoed out.

'Tell me about the call again,' I said to Jill.

Jill described what happened.

'Wish I'd heard it,' sighed Mum.

'Me too,' I said enviously.

Later, I whispered to Mum, 'You know, Jill must be very special to have heard that call.' Mum agreed. We both wondered what Jill's future held.

Nan had a very peaceful day. A happy day. The intense feeling that had surrounded our house for so long was gone, replaced by an overwhelming sense of calm.

At five-thirty the following morning, Ruth rang for an ambulance. Nan had insisted on it.

As they wheeled her out, she grasped Mum's hand one last time. There was an unspoken message in her eyes as she whispered, 'Leave my light burning for a few days.'

They placed her in the ambulance and Ruth climbed in beside her. Mum stood silently watching, accepting Nan's choice. Knowing that this was her final sacrifice. She wanted our old family home free of death.

My phone rang at seven that same morning.

'Sally? It's Ruth. Nan died twenty minutes ago. It was very peaceful.'

'Thanks,' I whispered.

I slowly replaced the receiver. I felt stiff. I couldn't move. Tears suddenly flooded my cheeks. For some reason, Jill's words from the previous day began echoing inside me. I heard the bird call, I heard the bird call. Around and around.

'Oh, Nan,' I cried with sudden certainty, 'I heard it, too. In my heart, I heard it.'